PRAISE FOR MARY KOLE

"Mary truly is amazing! Thanks to her, I have learned so much about writing. She made me laugh. She made me cry. She made me a better writer!" - *M. Churchill*

"I've read many books on the craft of writing, and *Writing Irresistible Kidlit* is among the best. I've never been so excited to get to the keyboard." - *Alan Harell*

"The advice is wonderful, thoughtful, and so clearly written that no writer could read Writing Irresistible Kidlit and not walk away with something gained from it." - *Ashlee W.*

"*Writing Irresistible Kidlit* is hands-down the best writing book I've read in years. It's a masterclass in a book." - *Alison S.*

"I can't begin to say how helpful *Writing Irresistible Kidlit* has been for my own writing journey." - *Joel A.*

"*Writing Irresistible Picture Books* is insightful, invaluable, and incredibly thorough! It's a must-have for anyone who aspires to write picture books and a great resource for those who are looking to hone their craft. I've already sent the link to writers I know." - *Elle*

"After writing a novel, unpublished writers inhabit an unguided middle space between not being important enough to warrant industry attention, and needing professional feedback to see how they stack up in the market. That is where Mary Kole lives. Her advice is sound, she pulls no punches, and if you listen to her, your work will improve." - *Andres Faza*

"Mary is a top professional in the industry and her advice is on-point and actionable. Having Mary on your team will no doubt improve your pitch, manuscript, query, or whatever you're writing." - *Elana I.*

"From now on, if I see a writing craft book with Mary Kole's name on it, I will hit the 'one click purchase' button without a second thought. She respects writers. She feels for writers. She understands writers. She knows exactly what insights writers need as they work. *Writing Irresistible Kidlit* is possibly the very best book on writing craft I have read in twenty-five years." - *Sprocket*

"*Writing Irresistible Kidlit* is quite simply, the best 'how to' book on novel writing that I've ever read and probably ever will read in my life." - *Carol*

"Mary Kole helped me to find my way. Her suggestions on my query letter are just what I needed to begin fearlessly searching for a place to call my own. I now consider Mary Kole my secret weapon." - *Tracy*

"Mary Kole brings years of solid experience and insight to the art of writing literature for younger audiences." - *Robin*

"*Writing Irresistible Kidlit* is the perfect blend of technical 'how to' guidance mixed with a healthy dose of encouragement. If anything I write in the future ever sells, I feel I may owe Ms. Kole a royalty for her shaping input from this book." - *A. Gable*

"I'm a big fan of everything Mary Kole does and this book was no exception. I learned so much reading Mary's feedback on the various components of each query letter in *Irresistible Query Letters*." - *Jamie L.*

"Kole is clearly passionate about her work and the world of kidlit, and that passion spills over the pages of *Writing Irresistible Kidlit*." - *Ashley B.*

"I would highly recommend learning from Mary Kole to anyone seriously looking to improve their writing." - *Kate K.*

"Receiving Mary's feedback on my novel has been one of the best things that has happened to my writing in recent years. Thanks to her, I see the possibilities in my book and also feel like a fire has been lit under me to continue. I know the work is not yet done, but today—*today*—I feel like it's possible."
- *Anonymous*

IRRESISTIBLE QUERY LETTERS WORKBOOK

by Mary Kole

GOOD STORY PUBLISHING

"Irresistible Query Letters Workbook"
By Mary Kole

1. Reference / Writing, Research, and Publishing Guides / Writing

FIRST EDITION
Print ISBN: 978-1-939162-12-0

Cover Design: Jenna Van Rooy
Layout and Formatting: Kaylee Pereyra

Printed in the United States of America

This workbook has been created to stand alone, but it's also a robust companion to *Irresistible Query Letters*, which features over forty real-life example queries with feedback on each:

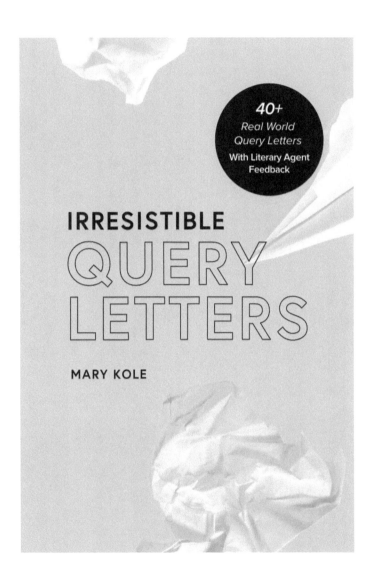

For Jenna Van Rooy: Amazing designer, brilliant mind,
partner in crime, certified cutie patootie, and dearest friend.

ABOUT MARY KOLE

As a former literary agent, Mary Kole knows the ins and outs of the publishing industry. She founded Mary Kole Editorial in 2013 to provide consulting and developmental editing services to writers across all categories and genres. She started Good Story Company in 2019 to create valuable content like the Good Story Podcast, Good Story YouTube channel, and the Writing Craft Workshop membership community. Her Story Mastermind small group workshop intensives help writers level up their craft, she offers done-for-you revision and ghostwriting with Manuscript Studio, and advises on marketing with Good Story Marketing.

She also develops unique and commercial intellectual property for middle grade, young adult, and adult readers with Upswell Media and Bittersweet Books, the latter with Folio Literary Management agent John Cusick and #1 *New York Times* best-selling author Julie Murphy.

Mary has appeared at regional, national, and international writing conferences for the SCBWI, Writer's Digest, Penn Writers, Writer's League of Texas, San Francisco Writers Conference, WIFYR, Writing Day, and many others. Her guest lectures have taken her to Harvard, the Ringling College of Art and Design, the Highlights Foundation, and more. Mary's recorded video classes can be found online at Writing Mastery Academy, Writing Blueprints, Udemy, and LinkedIn Learning.

Mary holds an MFA in Creative Writing and began her publishing career with a literary agency internship and the Kidlit blog, which she started in 2009. She has worked at Chronicle Books, the Andrea Brown Literary Agency, and Movable Type Management. Her books are *Writing Irresistible Kidlit: The Ultimate Guide to Crafting Fiction for Young Adult and Middle Grade Readers*, from Writer's Digest Books/Penguin Random House, and *Irresistible Query Letters*, *Writing Irresistible Picture Books*, the *Writing Irresistible Picture Books Workbook*, *How to Write a Book Now*, and *Writing Interiority*, from Good Story Publishing.

Originally from the San Francisco Bay Area, she lives with her three children, husband, two pugs, and a cat, in Minneapolis, MN.

TABLE OF CONTENTS

Introduction	1
Categories and Genres	7
Learning Your Options	9
Be Specific	21
Your Pitch	27
Fiction and Memoir Query Basics	35
The Query Meat	43
Other Types of Queries	63
Query Letter Formatting	79
The Synopsis	85
Query Voice and Writing Style!	91
Manuscript Formatting	95
Revising Your Query	99
Getting Feedback	111
Submission Best Practices	115
Submission Resources	122
Now What?	137
Staying Busy	153
Conclusion	157
Resources	159

INTRODUCTION

The query letter looms large in the writerly imagination. It always has. When I was a literary agent on the conference circuit—sometimes doing two or three large speaking events a month—I would marvel that nine out of ten questions from attendees in the audience seemed to be about *that dang query letter*. Not about the finer points of the writing craft. Not about publishing and career considerations. The trend was so pronounced that my fellow agents and I would gently laugh about it behind the scenes.

This always seemed a bit shortsighted, but I understood the rationale. To a writer hoping to break into print, the query letter seems like a powerful foot in the door. Besides, it's much easier to control (and obsess over!) a one-page document instead of a head-spinning three-hundred-page novel.

Queries are also mysterious. Most writers don't have a slush pile at their disposal, and rarely get the opportunity to glimpse what their peers are doing. Querying writers tend to keep their letters close to the vest due to superstition or self-doubt, especially as they approach submission with their projects. (Some also worry about idea theft, though these concerns are largely unfounded, as you'll see in an article in the resource section at the end of this workbook.)

If writers get meaningful feedback on their queries or manuscripts, they generally don't share this with peers outside of a writing group or workshop. How are most writers, then, supposed to level up their query craft?

The purpose of this workbook is to give you all the tools you need to confidently approach your own cover letter. Yes, that's right. The query is just a glorified cover letter, at the end of the day. When I was agenting, I would never offer representation based on the query alone. That's important to remember. The manuscript always, always came first.

Before we jump into deconstructing the components of a query letter and constructing your own, let's dream for a moment. Because that's—at least in part—what this whole writing endeavor is about, right?

WRITING DREAMS QUESTIONNAIRE

If you allow yourself to dream, what does a successful writing career look like for you?

Who are you writing for (other than your intended readers)?

- [ ] Myself
- [ ] A small group of friends and family
- [ ] For independent publication*
- [ ] For traditional publication
- [ ] Not sure yet!

What do you like most about writing?

*You won't need a query to self-publish, but you'll want to write marketing copy, which is similar. This workbook can still help!

WRITING DREAMS QUESTIONNAIRE

What is the nugget of inspiration that led you to explore your current WIP (work in progress)?

What are your short-term writing goals?

What are your long-term writing goals?

SUBMISSION HISTORY QUESTIONNAIRE

Have you been on submission before?

- ☐ Yes, but I wasn't successful
- ☐ Yes, but I now realize that I submitted too soon
- ☐ Yes, and I was successful, but am back in the trenches
- ☐ Not yet
- ☐ I'm about to submit and am doing last-minute prep!

What's your history with agents and publication?

- ☐ Not represented, not at all published
- ☐ Not agented, but have contracted directly with a publisher
- ☐ Was already published or represented, submitting again
- ☐ Independently published, looking to switch to traditional
- ☐ Only published in periodicals, working on a book
- ☐ I don't know what a lot of this means! (And that's okay!)

If you've been on submission before (to agents or publishers) or have been previously represented or published (indie or trad), what are your priorities this time around?

PROJECT TYPE QUESTIONNAIRE

Who is your target audience (category)?

☐ The youngest readers (board books, picture books, early readers)

☐ Independent readers (chapter books, middle grade)

☐ Young adults or new adults

☐ Adult readers

☐ I'm not sure—anyone and everyone!

What is the broad stylistic label for your work (genre)?

☐ Contemporary/realistic/literary

☐ High-concept/upmarket

☐ Fantasy/speculative/magical realism

☐ Action/adventure

☐ Science fiction

☐ Historical

☐ Horror

☐ Romance/romantic comedy

☐ Memoir/creative nonfiction

☐ Prescriptive nonfiction

☐ I'm not sure!

CATEGORIES AND GENRES

As you may have noticed on the previous page, I'm using the labels "category" and "genre" separately, which might be a bit confusing. This terminology is very intentional. "Category" refers to your intended target audience, for example, "the chapter book category." This is especially relevant in children's book publishing, where there are many different categories, and each has specific manuscript guidelines and expectations. "Genre" refers instead to content, for example, "the fantasy genre."

You can have a historical romance for adult readers, or a contemporary realistic novel for YA (young adult) readers. "Historical romance" and "contemporary realistic" are genre designations, and "adult" (used to differentiate it from children's books, not to denote adult content) and "YA" are categories.

It would be incorrect to call "picture book" a genre. It is a category. This small tweak can help you sound more professional in your pitch. Note that you can also mix genres—but generally not categories, as you'll want to settle on one target audience. (At least initially. There are projects that attain "crossover" status and get marketed to multiple reader demographics, but this is exceedingly rare and mostly orchestrated by publishers. This idea should not enter the conversation at the pitch stage.)

If this whole category/genre idea makes you chafe because you think labels are detrimental to your artistic freedom, know that these considerations are mostly for writers who want to publish traditionally. For better or worse, publishing is a business, and debut writers, especially, should think about where they (and their work) might fit. Categories and genres mirror bookstore shelves. Your work will need to go somewhere—they won't build you a custom podium at Barnes & Noble, unfortunately.

Trying to pitch something as appealing to "anyone and everyone" is aspirational, sure, but many publishers and agents might find this kind of statement naïve. Any marketer (and at some point, if you book is released as a product for sale, you will need to start thinking like a marketer) knows that you can't market one product to every person on the planet. The more specific your ideal reader—or "customer avatar"—the better your odds of hitting their unique tastes and expectations.

Watch out, also, for pitching that you have "something no one has ever done before." There could be a good reason why your genre-bending, category-busting 70,000-word picture book might not take off in the traditional market as it stands today (picture books generally have fewer than 600 words). Publishers may have tried it and learned it doesn't work the hard way. Or the potential audience for such a project might be too niche to target profitably.

As an aspiring debut writer, you have to play within the established writing and publishing rules before you might get more free rein to break them. At least, of course, if you're primarily interested in going the literary agent and traditional publisher route, which is what we'll talk about next.

LEARNING YOUR OPTIONS

When you're writing, you might not be paying close attention to the tastes of gatekeepers or the larger publishing industry around you, and that's okay. (The concept of "writing to market"—or creating a project with an eye on trends or a sense of what agents, publishers, and readers might be seeking —is controversial. Some writers love it, others feel that they can't express themselves as purely when they prioritize commerce. Follow your heart and your intentions on this one.)

When it comes time to submit your work, especially if you're aiming for traditional publication, you will want to solidify your market knowledge and learn more about the publishing landscape you hope to participate in. (Even if you end up self-publishing, know that the indie market is very trend-driven and you're better off if you understand it before you try to put yourself out there. All self-publishing platforms will ask you to apply categories and keywords to your work (whether their own or industry-standard BISAC codes), so you won't escape labels there, either.

PRO TIP: This workbook contains research and submission resources. Ideally, you are always going to be adding to your market knowledge by reading, interacting with online writing communities, and plugging into your local literary scene.

In this section, I'll show you how to get a stronger sense of market knowledge, as well as help you figure out if you want to approach a publisher directly, or try to get an agent first. (Or if you're better off independently publishing, though I strongly suggest you try to submit into the traditional system if you're *at all* curious before you DIY it. If you go right to independent publication but your heart is pining for a traditional book deal, you might always be wondering what might have been.)

Most Big Five publishers (HarperCollins, Penguin Random House, Hachette, Macmillan, and Simon & Schuster) will only take submissions through a literary agent who acts as an intermediary. There is one exception: If you meet an acquisitions editor at a conference or through another means of connection, they might open their submissions inbox directly to you as a courtesy, but usually for a short period of time.

There are also many small- to medium-sized publishing houses, regional presses, and academic publishers who'll take unagented submissions, so you can approach them directly (without an agent).

The submission and query process for both is the same, and I even advise writers to submit to agents *and* small publishers simultaneously, as there's very little chance of getting competing offers at the exact same moment (an offer of representation from an agent and a contract from a publisher).

So let's figure out if you want to query a **literary agent** or a **traditional publisher who takes unsolicited submissions**, or both.

PUBLISHER AND AGENT QUESTIONNAIRE

Not every project is a fit for a literary agent or major publisher. it's perfectly valid to publish with a niche, educational, institutional, regional, or academic publisher and contract with them directly. That said, if you work with an agent, you should be prepared to give up 15% of your gross revenue as a commission on domestic deals (foreign and film deals often involve a co-agent and the commission can be higher, between 20% and 25%). If you contract directly with a publisher, know that they will negotiate in *their* best interest. (It's not malicious, it's just business.) Make sure to run any proposed publishing contract by an IP or entertainment lawyer before agreeing to terms or signing, as you might be bound to that house and those contractual stipulations for the term of copyright (your life plus seventy years).

01

I've decided to submit to: YES   NO
                                                              ☐   ☐

- ☐ Agents only
- ☐ Small- to medium-sized publishers only
- ☐ A mix of both

02

I believe my project is a fit for a major   YES   NO
agency or publisher. If yes, here's why: ☐   ☐

- ☐ I believe it has a marketable hook
- ☐ I've found comparative titles that sold well
- ☐ I have a sales record but might have a breakout on my hands
- ☐ I don't know, but I want to try!

11

IDEAL AGENT QUESTIONNAIRE

If you're considering of approaching agents directly, take some time to think about what you want your ideal agent-author relationship to be. You might not get your exact your wish, or your expectations might be unreasonable for what's considered industry standard, but if you haven't percolated on these issues before, you'll want to check in with yourself, and sooner rather than later.

What's important to you in an agent-author relationship? (If you've already had an agent or multiple agents before, what would you like to have happen differently this time around?)

01

I know my ideal communication style.

YES ☐   NO ☐

☐ I largely like being left to my own devices

☐ I appreciate frequent check-ins and hand-holding

☐ I adapt to others' communication styles

I prefer the following:

☐ Email ☐ Phone ☐ Carrier Pigeon/Leave Me Alone Unless There's an Offer

☐ Text ☐ Video

I realize both "editorial" and hands-off agents exist. I'd prefer to work with:

YES ☐   NO ☐

02

☐ A highly editorial agent

☐ Someone who gives market advice but lets me do the art

☐ Someone who gives me creative autonomy

---

03 Does size of agency or NYC location matter to me? If so, what are my priorities for an agency's prestige or clout? *How much* does this matter?

YES ☐   NO ☐

Not all agencies and agents are created equal in terms of reputation, strengths, contacts with publishers, sales history, and interests. The business is TRULY subjective. In fact, anyone can hang a shingle out and call themselves an agent. That's why vetting your potential submission targets, which I'll discuss at length later in this workbook, is such a good idea.

REMEMBER: You are hiring *them*. That's right. This can be tough to imagine and even tougher to believe (most writers just want someone, *anyone*, to say "yes")! But your desires and priorities absolutely factor into this equation.

IDEAL PUBLISHER QUESTIONNAIRE

If you're thinking of approaching publishers directly, the submission process is largely the same as it is for agents. (We'll dive into submission best practices starting on page 117.) Be aware that not every publisher is equal, and most of the publishing houses you'll find by Googling "publisher for my book" (or similar) will be "hybrid" or "pay to play" business models, where you will be offered a contract, then quickly asked to pay production and promotion costs. Unless you're explicitly sure that you want to work with a vanity or hybrid publisher, you should stay away from these too-good-to-be-true offers. There are plenty of traditional houses that work directly with writers, you just have to find them and reach out (more on this on pages 122 and 123).

What appeals to you about working directly with a publishing partner?

01 Are you content to skip submission to a major house?

YES ☐ NO ☐

02 If you publish directly (without an agent), would you try to use it as a stepping stone? (It's also perfectly valid to stay with a smaller publisher for good.)

YES ☐ NO ☐

03
Is this an intentional strategy on your part? (If not, and you are submitting directly to publishers because you don't feel you can find a home elsewhere, you might want to hone your craft more, as submitting due to lack of confidence isn't a strong play.)

YES ☐   NO ☐

04
Do you have more than one project in you as a writer? (If so, forming a direct relationship with an editor at a publishing house can be a good strategy.)

YES ☐   NO ☐

05
Are you only submitting directly to save agency commission? If so, see below.

YES ☐   NO ☐

PRO TIP:
I'm a former literary agent, so you might expect me to be an automatic booster for agents. Not so! Hiring an agent doesn't make sense for some projects, which might be a better fit for a small house. That said, making short-sighted decisions to save a 15% commission might not pay off in the long run. Agents are often able to negotiate bigger or more advantageous deals, so 85% of a higher advance (compared to what you might be able to achieve yourself) might be a stronger number than 100% of a smaller advance.

MARKET LEARNING CHECKLIST

It's never been easier to learn what your competition (meant in a friendly way) is doing. All around you are authors writing at the top of their game. You can also get remarkable insights into books that aren't going to be published for a year or two (see the resources on pages 122 and 123). This said, there's no excuse not to dive in and learn the industry that you hope to be a part of.

01 I've visited the library or independent bookstore and browsed some potential comparative titles (more about those on page 37) that have been published within the **last three years**.

YES ☐ NO ☐

Five titles I noticed in my category/genre:
1.
2.
3.
4.
5.

02 I've started paying more attention to future books that are coming out, especially those in my genre and category.

YES ☐ NO ☐

Two upcoming publishing deals that interested me:
1.
2.

A trend I'm noticing in the market, especially in my category and/or genre, is:

How does my WIP relate to this potential trend?

How unique is my project (while still fitting into this slice of the market)? How can I further distinguish myself?

WORD COUNT EXPECTATIONS

While you're learning the market, it might be helpful to get acquainted with broad-strokes conventions for word count. There are many websites that feature ideas for genre tropes and expectations—one of my favorites for various character and plot points is TVTropes.org, which bills itself as "an all-devouring pop-culture wiki." Love it or hate it, our media landscape is becoming more and more commodified, so if you're consciously playing with some of these elements, you might make yourself more attractive to the larger and more commercial agents and publishing houses. All this said, there are definitely expectations for each genre and category, and one of the the most visible is **word count**. Having an obviously incongruent word count at the top of your query letter can absolutely make a gatekeeper bounce immediately.

CHILDREN'S BOOKS:

Children's publishing is its own beast, and books for young readers tend to be very regimented in terms of word count and other guidelines (word choice, syntax, chapter length, etc.). You may not agree with these standards, but by ignoring them, you are likely hamstringing your submission, especially as an aspiring debut.

- Board Books (ages zero to three): >100 words
- Younger Picture Books (ages three to five): >400 words
- Older Picture Books (ages five to seven): >600 words
- Younger Nonfiction Picture Books: >1,500 words
- Older Nonfiction Picture Books: >3,000 words
- Early Readers (ages six to eight)> 1,500 words
- Chapter Books (ages seven to nine): 5,000 to 15,000 words

CHILDREN'S BOOKS (CONT.):

- Younger Middle Grade (ages nine to eleven): 35,000 to 50,000 words
- Older Middle Grade (ages eleven to thirteen, including fantasy and adventure): 50,000 to 80,000 words
- Young Adult (ages fourteen+): 50,000 to 80,000 words
- Older Young Adult (ages sixteen+, including fantasy, historical, sci-fi): 70,000 to 120,000 words

BOOKS FOR ADULT READERS:

- Contemporary Fiction: 60,000 words and up
- Memoir: 60,000 words and up
- Romance/Romantic Comedy: 60,000 words and up
- Literary Fiction: 80,000 words and up
- Fantasy, Sci-Fi, Speculative, and Historical: 80,000 words and up, but can go comfortably to about 120,000 before raising eyebrows
- Nonfiction: 70,000 words and up (depending on the topic)

PRO TIP: Exceptions exist to every rule. You have them on your bookshelf right now and can easily find something to contradict these broad-strokes guidelines. That's fine. But in contemporary publishing, a debut writer is better served trying to fit into established guidelines rather than breaking the rules the first time out. Yes, this is antithetical to the very nature of art. But some writers want to publish because they envision commercial success for themselves. As such, these concepts are most relevant if you want to attract a literary agent and major publisher.

Before you begin to write your own pitch, let's do one more exercise.

BE SPECIFIC

Specificity is key in a pitch. It's very unusual for a gatekeeper to understand what your story is truly about—and what your unique value propositions are—if you don't communicate your character, plot, or world-building (if applicable, see page 54) in specific terms. (While this section is geared to fiction memoir pitches, specificity is required for all pitches.) To illustrate this point, let's see a vague pitch first.

VAGUE EXAMPLE:

> *He takes a meaningful journey to a harrowing place where he fights injustice and rights the wrongs of his enemies, finally coming to peace with himself.*

This could literally be any story, as it transcribes Joseph Campbell's Hero's Journey beats.

NOW, MAKE IT SPECIFIC:

> *He discovers that he is a demi-god and is thrust into a world of temperamental gods, who've made him their scapegoat. He journeys literally to hell and back to keep Hades from killing him and to win the favor of his father, Poseidon.*

This can *only* be *Percy Jackson and the Lightning Thief* by Rick Riordan.

Now, you'll notice that the specific example is longer. But see how much more information it contains? That's key. We know what the fantasy world-building elements are (Greek gods and demi-gods), we know the basic shape of the plot (journey to hell and back), we know the external conflict (the gods are at war), and the internal conflict for the protagonist (he's hoping to impress his father).

None of that is evident in the vague example, though it could also, technically, describe the basic gist of *Percy Jackson and the Lightning Thief*.

If you were completely new to this particular book, which pitch would you like to read to evaluate whether or not you'd like it (or even understand the broad strokes)? The specific one, most likely. The vague pitch goes in one ear and out the other. I don't know about you, but I couldn't possibly repeat it back to you, not even immediately after hearing it. And I wrote it!

Such is the power of specificity.

Now, I want you to take a crack at it! For the following examples, if you're not familiar with the published story referenced, go online and read a summary. I'd prefer if you went to the horse's mouth and examined the publisher's official marketing copy, rather than an amateur review. This is the text that appears as the book's description wherever the book is sold online or the publisher's own website. (Reading marketing materials will train your brain to notice how to entice readers when pitching story. That's what query letter-writing is!)

Remember to try and capture the spark—the uniqueness and sales hook—of the project. Most of the following books are well-known and beloved. How might you convey that in a short and specific statement?

SPECIFICITY WORKSHEET

VAGUE EXAMPLE #1:

A contest between children from various districts will determine sovereignty in this society, but multiple players will have to make the ultimate sacrifice.

Now tune it to *The Hunger Games* **by Suzanne Collins:**

VAGUE EXAMPLE #2:

An underdog learns to triumph over adversity by standing up for herself and owning her truth.

Now tune it to *Lessons in Chemistry* **by Bonnie Garmus:**

VAGUE EXAMPLE #3:

Two publishing professionals disagree about all things, including matters of the heart.

Now tune it to *Book Lovers* **by Emily Henry:**

VAGUE EXAMPLE #4:

An underdog must earn her keep in an army that uses dragons for warfare.

Now tune it to *Fourth Wing* **by Rebecca Yarros:**

VAGUE EXAMPLE #5:

A change in the world means a father and son must go on the road.

Now tune it to *The Road* **by Cormac McCarthy***:*

VAGUE EXAMPLE #6:

A change in family structure offers represents a major shift for a young man.

Now tune it to *A Heartbreaking Work of Staggering Genius* **by Dave Eggers (try to capture the tone and voice!):**

Now that you've thought about your project, the market, and whether you might want to submit to a literary agent, directly to a publisher, or both, let's formulate your logline.

PSST: Even if you're not writing a memoir or fiction project, have a read through all of the following sections anyway because they will define some key terms and query letter ingredients. I'll cover special case queries (for illustrated projects and nonfiction) on page 63.

YOUR PITCH

As you'll see in a moment, having a pitch, mission statement, or any other kind of one- or two-line summary of your project is optional. You might find, however, that developing a logline will help you write the query. This is the hardest part for a lot of writers—to distill their work into the shortest possible morsel. That's okay. You aren't the first person to think queries are a draconian exercise.

Whether you end up using this pitch or not, you'll have to answer the question "What's your book about?" at some point. You'll have to do it *a lot*, in fact, once you become published. The sooner you get comfortable with this contrivance, the better.

Here are some logline best practices:
- A logline can rely on your comps ("It's *Sharknado* meets *Water for Elephants*") or you can write a one-or-two sentence pitch (maximum!) that summarizes your story.
- You can also ask a "What if?" question. ("What if two teens from rival families fell in love?" That's *Romeo and Juliet*.)
- Another approach is to write two sentences that emphasize your character's driving narrative arc and the heart of the plot. For example, "A girl must fight a group of teenagers to the death to save her own sister and redeem her country." (This is *The Hunger Games*.)

- Don't skimp on the high drama of your story. The logline is where it should come out to play. I'll discuss this in more detail in the query meat section on page 43.

PITCHING PICTURE BOOKS:

You'll want to keep your pitch short, focusing on your character and main plot conflict. (Yes, picture books need to have conflict, though it's often empowering in nature, since the solution is spearheaded by the kid character.)

But not every picture book is a narrative project. There are concept and nonfiction picture books as well. For those, you'll want to focus on your topic and what makes your particular slant unique, similar to my advice for adult nonfiction work, below.

PITCHING NONFICTION:

A nonfiction logline should be quite simple: Why is your take on the subject new and different, and why do people want/need it right now? An example could be: "Simon Sinek got it wrong about 'starting with why.' You actually need to start with *how*." This logline references a bestselling nonfiction thought leadership project but subverts expectations as well, which might tantalize a reader into wanting to know more.

FICTION AND MEMOIR LOGLINE WORKSHEET

A logline for fiction, memoir, and narrative picture book generally includes only the barest minimum ingredients:

- The protagonist
- The main conflict or climactic action
- The theme or bigger picture exploration of the project

Who is my primary protagonist?

What is the biggest conflict they face?

What is my thematic exploration or mission statement for the book?

TRY A LOGLINE DRAFT:

_____

_____

_____

_____

_____

_____

_____

_____

_____

_____

_____

_____

_____

_____

_____

_____

_____

_____

NOW TRY A "MEETS" COMPARISON WITH COMPS:

_____

_____

_____

_____

_____

_____

TRY A "WHAT IF?" FORMAT:

_____

_____

_____

_____

_____

_____

NONFICTION LOGLINE WORKSHEET

The logline for nonfiction generally includes only the barest minimum ingredients:

- Your unique slant on your specific topic
- Why a large audience will be into *this* particular treatment of said topic
- Why you're the expert to bring *this* slant to *this* market **now**

What's my unique slant on a popular topic?

Why does my audience need this new treatment of said topic?

Why am I the expert to bring this to market now?

TRY A LOGLINE DRAFT:

NOW TRY A "MEETS" COMPARISON WITH COMPS:

_____

_____

_____

_____

_____

_____

TRY A "WHAT IF?" FORMAT:

_____

_____

_____

_____

_____

_____

Now let's dive into the query letter itself!

FICTION AND MEMOIR QUERY BASICS

The query is a 200-400-word **cover letter**, as alluded to in the introduction. While many writers obsess over the query (and, more recently, over that comparative title sentence), I promise you that I never, ever, *ever* offered representation to a writer based on their query alone when I was a literary agent.

The manuscript is always infinitely more important. The query's job is to whet a gatekeeper's whistle and make them excited to read the writing sample (or complete manuscript, for picture book, or book proposal, for nonfiction, which we'll talk about on page 63).

The stronger and clearer your pitch, the more excited they'll be. Once you're sure that you're pitching your work and yourself in a compelling way, you can trust that the query is doing its job. There are tons of forces in the market (and in an individual agent or acquiring editor's mind) that you can't control. Your job is to study the landscape around you, learn your craft, and then control what you can—your pitch and your project.

Of course, you're here for query information, so let's spell out the basic ingredients of your fiction or memoir letter. This is the most common kind of letter that writers are curious about.

OPTIONAL QUERY INGREDIENTS:

The following query components are great if you have them, but a potential liability if you don't (or do them wrong, as there are ways to strike out with these). If you choose to use these, note that they're often expected to appear at the beginning of the query.

- **Personalization**
  - If you have a specific personal reason for contacting the agent or publisher, mention it. For example, "I'm querying you because you represented my favorite book, *Title*." This speaks to that agent or publisher's experience.
  - If you want to remind the gatekeeper of a previous interaction, that's always relevant, too. For example, "I'm querying you because we met at (Name of Writing Conference in Month, Year), and you requested the first ten pages of my work." If you have it, use it!
  - An example of bad personalization would be, "I'm querying you because of your passion for literature." This is vague and can be said of anyone working in the book business. Agents and publishers, of all people, can recognize a form letter. So if this is the best you have to offer, omit the personalization element.
  - Your best weapon here is strong research to find connection points with the people you're querying, if at all possible. (A word of warning here: Depending on how deeply you dive into researching various gatekeepers, you may find personal information, like individual social media, children's names, etc. Only use these details if you are sure you're hitting an appropriate tone. The more personal you get, the easier it is to come off as downright creepy.)

- ## Comparative Titles ("Comp Titles")
  - If you find that you have something in common with books or authors already on shelves, feel free to use comp titles to bolster your pitch.
  - It's important to remember that the comp title section is optional, especially if you don't have anything compelling to put there.
  - Many writers seem to be increasingly convinced that comparative titles are some kind of secret code that will unlock a manuscript request. Not true, but they're nice to use if you're able to find good ones.
  - Comps should be within your category and genre, whenever possible.
  - They should also be **recent**, which means published within the last three years.
  - You should conspicuously avoid comping to bestselling authors or projects, as this can convey unrealistic expectations.
  - You can compare your work to an *element* from a comp title, such as, "With the witty banter of Emily Henry, and the thrilling twists of Riley Sager ..."
  - See the Resources section on page 159 for more thoughts on comps.

- ## Logline/Pitch
  - If you're already using personalization and comp titles, you can skip the logline that you developed in the previous section. Remember that loglines are largely optional, because you are going to be pitching the story in much more detail in the following paragraphs anyway.
  - However, some writers really like to start with a punchy sentence or two. This is a stylistic choice.
  - You can also practice writing your own logline or premise statement to focus your thought process during writing or revision. (You'll also see this referred to as a "pitch," "elevator pitch," or similar. All of these terms mean a short expression of what your book is about.)

REQUIRED QUERY INGREDIENTS:

Once you start crafting your query in earnest, there are certain elements that you must include for your letter to be seen as competent, competitive, and compelling (all good things!).

- **Manuscript Logistics**
  - This is where you mention the title, genre, category, word count, and anything else relevant to your manuscript itself, like any unusual narrative choices. For example, "TITLE is a 51,000-word middle grade fantasy manuscript told in second person direct address," or, "Told in dual narrative POV, TITLE is a 75,000-word literary novel in verse." The title, word count, and target audience are the bare minimum here.
  - This statement will help gatekeepers tune their expectations. If they don't learn until the end of your query that you're intending the story to be a fantasy for young readers, they may have to go back and re-evaluate everything with that knowledge in mind.
  - Make it easy for the agent or publisher to set expectations and give them the basics so they can read ahead confidently.
  - This is also a great litmus test for whether you know what you're doing because you will want your word count, genre expectations, and category to line up with current market conventions. If they don't, a gatekeeper might have less confidence in your skills and market knowledge.

- **Query Meat**
  - The heart of the query is the query meat, which I'll unpack it in more detail in the following section. What you'll learn pertains specifically to fiction and memoir projects, and really helps you make a case for engaging gatekeepers.
  - The meat should be between one and three paragraphs long and will present the character and plot of your narrative.
  - You'll also convey a sense of tone and world-building (if applicable). We'll talk a lot more about the query meat in a moment.

- **Bio Paragraph**
  - This section is all about you. It's strange when this component is entirely missing, so think of at least one sentence to include. On the other hand, don't go overboard with voice, jokes, or personality.
  - Don't make your bio longer than the query meat.

- **Bio Paragraph (cont.)**
  - Include only professional-sounding and relevant details. If you have writing credits, publications, or competition wins or placements, make sure to cite specifics (publisher and year, for example).
  - Make sure to format periodicals, literary journals, published titles, and any TV or movie projects (if applicable) in italics. (Unpublished manuscript titles are generally formatted either in all caps or using double quotation marks throughout.)
  - If you aren't presenting your publications, contest wins, or clips (other published pieces) professionally, gatekeepers will assume that you self-published your previous work or entered contests where everyone who pays the fee gets a "prize." If this is the case, say so. There really is no shame about these choices, but hiding parts of your resume or spinning the truth might land you in trouble.
  - Finally, avoid being too cheeky in this section. The number of cats you have is probably not going to be relevant, unless you are writing a cat book. Focus on your literary education (if any), publishing credentials (if any), and life experience that's related to the project at hand.

AND FINALLY...

You will want to include a breezy sign-off. For memoir and fiction, it can literally be the following:

> *Per your guidelines, the first (# of pages or chapters) are pasted below. Please note that this is a simultaneous submission. Thank you very much for your time and consideration.*

- **Signature**
  - The final component of your query letter is exactly what it sounds like. Your real name, a pen name (if you're using one), your contact information (ideally email and phone number, minimum, but you can include your mailing address), and any online credentials like your website URL and social media profiles. These can all go underneath the letter on separate lines.

And that's it for our fiction and memoir query basics! I'll talk about the query meat next, then I'll cover special case queries (illustrated projects and nonfiction). After that, I'll go into preferred query formatting, so you know you'll be arranging everything in the right order!

FYI FOR MEMOIRS:

It's important to note that most memoirs (unless your last name is Kardashian, or similar) are sold as complete manuscripts these days, which represents a change of protocol. Memoirs used to be sold on proposal, with only a few sample chapters needed, but they have more in common with fiction on the submission side.

You will find confusing information about memoir submission online. Memoirs are technically nonfiction, even if they fall into the category of "narrative nonfiction" or "creative nonfiction."

However, you will still see some memoir submission guidelines on various publisher and literary agency websites asking for a proposal. Some websites do not explicitly mention anything other than fiction and nonfiction, even though logistically speaking, memoir occupies a gray area between the two.

For fiction, submission guidelines will generally ask for a query, synopsis (sometimes), and first ten pages/three chapters/etc. (Every submission guideline is, frustratingly, different.) For nonfiction, they will ask for a query, proposal, and associated sample chapters.

If you're writing a memoir and only have a proposal, though, you're in trouble. They'll expect a full manuscript. Even if you submit a proposal and someone is interested, the agent will ask for a complete manuscript shortly thereafter. You must have one.

Therefore, it's better to have the following documents prepared before you submit a memoir:

1. **Query Letter**
2. **Synopsis**
3. **Short Proposal (and up to three sample chapters)**
4. **Complete Manuscript**

This way, you can send whatever configuration they request. While it might be too early to talk about submitting your work, you need to know what's ahead so there are no surprises ahead.

In the following section, we will do a deep dive into the query meat—the detailed pitch for your fiction picture book, novel, or memoir.

THE QUERY MEAT

Whether you pitch an agent in person or with a written query, your goal is the same: to get the gatekeeper to request your manuscript. And you can usually do that by framing your story in a way that makes your audiences care. If you answer the following questions about your fiction or memoir manuscript, you're sure to hit a framework that practically demands an emotional response.

Here's an example of query meat, written for the young adult romantasy (a portmanteau of "romance" and "fantasy") novel, *Fourth Wing* by Rebecca Yarros:

WHO IS YOUR CHARACTER?

> *Violet Sorrengail is all set for a quiet life as a cloistered scribe, a vocation where her "fragile" body won't be a problem.*

WHAT IS THE INCITING INCIDENT?

In other words: What is the strange thing going on in their life that throws everything off-kilter and launches the story?

> *Then her mother—the general of Navarre—issues a life-changing command: that Violet must follow her siblings and try to become a dragon rider. Emphasis on* try.

WHAT IS THEIR OBJECTIVE?

In other words: What (or who) do they want most in the world?

> *Most cadets die before they bond with a dragon, so Violet must prove her strength to them … and herself.*

WHAT IS THEIR OBSTACLE?

In other words: Who (or what) is in the way of them getting what they want?

> *Worse, everyone seems to hate Violet for who her mother is … and what her family did during the rebellion. Nobody's more fired up to kill her than red-hot Xaden Riorson, her wingleader.*

WHAT'S AT STAKE?

What does the character risk, or what might they lose (internally and externally) if their plan fails or they don't get what they want?

> *Tensions soar when Violet actually bonds ... with two dragons, an unprecedented feat. One of them is tied to Xaden's dragon, throwing the two ever closer together. But her problems are just beginning. Now every unbonded rider wants to kill her and take her place. And they haven't even gone to war yet.*

WHERE'S THE HOOK?

This is a catch-all for any especially high-concept or appealing element of the story that seals the deal in terms of any intrigue your premise offers. While I'll argue later for revealing any twists, you can also dangle a curiosity hook.

> *As battle heats up, Violet must hold on tight—or fall out of the sky. Except there are greater forces at work on the battlefield and in the chain of command. These betrayals will call into question everything Violet knows, and everything she flies for.*

ONCE MORE, FROM THE TOP:

Violet Sorrengail is all set for a quiet life as a cloistered scribe, a vocation where her "fragile" body won't be a problem. Then her mother—the general of Navarre—issues a life-changing command: that Violet must follow her siblings and try to become a dragon rider. Emphasis on try. Most cadets die before they bond with a dragon, so Violet must prove her strength to them … and herself.

Worse, everyone seems to hate Violet for who her mother is … and what happened during the rebellion. Nobody's more fired up to kill her than red-hot Xaden Riorson, her wingleader. Tensions soar when Violet actually bonds … with two dragons, an unprecedented feat. One of them is tied to Xaden's dragon, throwing the two ever closer together. But her problems are just beginning. Now every unbonded rider wants to kill her and take her place. And they haven't even gone to war yet.

PRO TIP: You'll notice that this query meat spans two paragraphs. I've omitted a lot of detail here. You might want to end up with one to three solid paragraphs of information, especially if your story is world-building heavy, like fantasy, historical, and science fiction projects tend to be.

Also, I could've easily omitted mention of Xaden here, but I included the love interest to suggest an enemies-to-lovers trope and to add romance content. Otherwise, a pitch without Xaden would set mostly fantasy expectations, rather than romantasy, which was having a very trendy moment when this novel was released.

Next, we'll talk about special considerations for fiction and memoir queries.

MULTIPLE NARRATORS

What if you have multiple narrators in your project? That can be a challenging narrative choice, as well as a challenging query letter to write. A fiction or memoir query writer's job is to sell the reader on a compelling story. This gets more complicated when you have multiple characters to cover each, with their own development and maybe even plot arcs.

Focus on how the characters come together and any conflicts between them. Weave in plot points they share in common. Are the various character perspectives rendered in alternating chapters? Are their plots interrelated (most common)? Or do we go from POV to POV using another organizing principle? Be sure to mention that yours is a multiple POV project in the logistical portion at the top of the query. Any time a writer uses a different storytelling style, that's relevant information for the agent or publisher to know right away.

PRO TIP: Run your multi-POV query letter by a reader who has no idea what your story is about. Ask them who the main character is. Ask them to describe the thrust of your story back to you. If they can't, that tells you something.

This is a good thing to do even if you're writing a single POV. If someone can get the gist of your project from the query, you are going to be far ahead of others in the slush pile!

REVEALING THE TWIST

The query is a pitching/teasing document that wants to cultivate engagement and excitement. But if you have a big twist in your story, **reveal it**! That's right. No agent or acquisitions editor is going to request a full manuscript and read it for five hours just because you tantalize them with one rhetorical question. Nobody has that kind of time, and curiosity is not that strong a motivator. Tell them *what* you do in the story, and they'll be excited to see *how* you do it.

Answer the questions in the following questionnaires and checklists about your own manuscript. Read the back and jacket flap copy of published books. By doing this, you will start to internalize the length and tone you're aiming for with a verbal pitch or the meat of your written query.

The most well-crafted queries, in my opinion, are ones that make me care about the story and characters. They make me feel something. They make me want to know what happens next.

Agents and editors want to hear from writers. They want good projects. They simply can't do their jobs without them.

So present the juiciest, most compelling points of your story, mention the important details outlined above, and, finally, keep it in perspective. Query letters are just cover letters. They're tasty little appetizers.

Now, you try it! That's right. Take your first stab at constructing your query letter. We'll start by focusing in on your protagonist—the star of the fiction or memoir show.

HONE YOUR PROTAGONIST

Remember, a "pitch," "logline," and "elevator pitch" are related terms for a quick written or verbal summary of your story, meant to be communicated in an enticing way. While the terms and definitions can differ, the point of a pitch is the same: To make listeners or readers want to know more. A good fiction or memoir query starts with character, so let's identify some key elements that you'll need to include.

To write a compelling pitch, you need to think about what your character wants (objective), why they want it (motivation), and maybe even their underlying need or driver (more vulnerable than a superficial objective). What are the stakes that threaten their objective, motivation, and/or need?

If you've done your writing homework, you should have no problem isolating these concepts. If you're stumped by some of these questions, you might be premature in your desire to submit. Check out my character writing guide, *Writing Interiority: Crafting Irresistible Characters* for an incredibly deep dive into all things protagonist.

My character's objective is:

My character's motivation is:

My character's need is:

It's important for your character to be **proactive**. The plot shouldn't happen **to** your character. The protagonist should **make** the plot happen through their desires, actions, and choices. (A passive character often emerges as an issue at the query stage!)

Some actions that make my character proactive are:

What's the biggest obstacle my character faces?

Who/what is the antagonizing force in the story?

The character's stakes are:

Any other information about your character that the gatekeeper **absolutely needs to know**:

HONE YOUR PLOT

Now that your protagonist (or multiple protagonists, see page 46) is established, you'll need to give them something to do. Even in the query, your main character will ideally come across as proactive, especially since you've given them an objective, motivation, need, and stakes.

Not all stories have to follow the same format, but remember—we're going for emotional engagement from a reader who's evaluating hundreds of pitches in one sitting. Knowing who a character is and what they want—then putting that against the backdrop of the story's plot and world—will give your gatekeeper a strong sense of what your book is about. If you find yourself struggling to name some of these plot and conflict elements, you might have a story problem, not a query problem. Even the "quietest" literary pieces need some kind of driving external conflict to provide a sense of structure.

What type of conflict does your narrative feature?

01

- [ ] Character vs. other character/antagonist
- [ ] Character vs. society
- [ ] Character vs. larger world antagonist
- [ ] Character vs. betrayal
- [ ] Character vs. self
- [ ] Character vs. their past

Is your conflict **acute** or **chronic** (new or ongoing)?

02

- [ ] Acute
- [ ] Chronic

03 Is your conflict **internal** or **external**?
(The character grapples within themselves OR with an event or situation that acts upon your character from the outside.)

- ☐ Internal
- ☐ External
- ☐ Both

---

04 There's a clear reason why the story starts **today**, as opposed to yesterday or next week (remember your inciting incident).

YES ☐ NO ☐

---

05 The events of the story flow in a cause-and-effect sequence, rather than happening seemingly randomly. This progression is clear in the query.

YES ☐ NO ☐

---

06 The beginning of the query seems to circle back to the end or refer to the opening conflict in some way. (If the query takes a left turn, this might be harder to follow.)

YES ☐ NO ☐

---

07 My query has a good balance of:

YES ☐ NO ☐

- ☐ Character description
- ☐ Objective/motivation
- ☐ Antagonism/obstacles
- ☐ Sense of stakes
- ☐ Deeper impact on character

STORY STRUCTURE CHECKLIST

01 My story has a definite beginning, middle, and end. YES ☐ NO ☐

02 There is conflict introduced in the first few pages. YES ☐ NO ☐

03 Characters have tension or conflict with one another, rather than simply coexisting. This conflict drives the story forward. YES ☐ NO ☐

04 The story incorporates stakes, or a reason why the story matters to the character (and therefore the reader). YES ☐ NO ☐

05 The initial conflict either escalates throughout, or the conflict transforms or transitions around the midpoint. YES ☐ NO ☐

06 The story has an engaging resolution that's hinted at in the query or outright revealed to showcase your storytelling imagination. YES ☐ NO ☐

There's obviously a whole lot more to it, but you want to make sure these broad-strokes story elements are in place before you go about pitching your story.

QUERY WORLD-BUILDING WORKSHEET

What are the unique elements of your speculative or historical world (if applicable)that make your book stand out?

How do you describe them in the query?

How do these elements directly impact the main character?

How do these elements directly impact the plot?

What's the logic of why the magic/society works as it does?

STORY ELEMENTS CHECKLIST

01 There are **no more than three** named characters, or characters who readers will need to follow throughout the query.

YES ☐   NO ☐

My story's secondary characters, including the antagonist:
1
2
3

02 It's clear why these other characters are needed in the query because they contribute to the conflict (spotlight the villain, if applicable).

YES ☐   NO ☐

To summarize and reiterate, the conflict between characters is:

03 I focus mostly on the protagonist's character arc and development (unless I have to track multiple POVs).

YES ☐   NO ☐

04   My setting affects both character and plot.   YES ☐   NO ☐

My setting is:

05   I've included a sense of the main events of the plot, such as the inciting incident, midpoint transformation, and climactic action.   YES ☐   NO ☐

Three main story events featured in the query are:
1
2
3

06   I've hinted at or outright revealed the climactic twist (especially in a thriller or mystery) rather than teasing it.   YES ☐   NO ☐

07   If my setting has fantasy/magical/historical elements, there's a very clear story- and theme-based reason why they exist, and I've expressed what makes my speculative elements original or unique.   YES ☐   NO ☐

Now let's put all of these elements together!

BUILD YOUR QUERY LETTER

PERSONALIZATION*:

If you have a personal reason for contacting a specific agent or publisher, use it! You'll get some specific data with your agent and publisher research (see pages 122 and 123) and find space to track personalization for all of your targets later in this workbook.

> For example: "I'm querying you because you represented my favorite book, *Title*."

COMPARATIVE TITLES*:

If you find that your work has something in common with books or authors already on shelves, feel free to reference up to three recent comp titles (published within the last three years).

1
2
3

*These elements are optional, but may help you stand out in the slush pile.

LOGLINE*:

Pick your favorite pitch from the previous section.

[   ]

MANUSCRIPT LOGISTICS:

This section of the query is where you mention the title, word count, and anything else relevant to your manuscript.

The title and word count are the bare minimum here.

For example: "TITLE is a 75,000-word upmarket book club novel."

[   ]

*These elements are optional,
but may help you stand out in the slush pile.

THE QUERY MEAT:

The most substantial part of the query is the one- or three-paragraph description that presents the character and plot of your narrative project.

- Focus on character, plot, any interesting or timely sales hooks and the universal theme or outcome.
- Read the backs of published books and their sales page marketing copy. This is roughly the length and tone you're going for.
- Keep your query letter to 300 words, or up to one single-spaced page. If you're beyond 400 words, this is unusual (and likely unnecessary), unless you're writing multi-POV/fantasy/sci-fi/historical.

_____

_____

_____

_____

_____

_____

_____

_____

_____

_____

_____

_____

THE QUERY MEAT (CONT.):

_____

_____

_____

_____

_____

_____

_____

_____

_____

_____

_____

_____

_____

_____

_____

BIOGRAPHICAL INFO:

This refers to information about you and your qualifications or writing experience.

> **Don't make your bio longer than the query meat.** Include only professional-sounding and relevant details. Make sure to cite your publication or contest names and years, if relevant. Italicize book, journal, and periodical titles.

QUERY LOGISTICS:

This is your breezy sign-off to the query letter itself.

> **It can literally be the following:** *Per your guidelines, the first ten pages are enclosed below. Please note that this is a simultaneous submission. Thank you very much for your time and consideration.*

NAME AND SIGNATURE:

Don't overcomplicate it, and don't hide your true identity, even if you plan to use a pen name.

Your real name:
Your pen name (if you're using one):
Best contact info (email and phone number, at minimum):
Website URLs or social media profiles:

THAT'S IT?

Yes! You'll want to revise and refine it a few times, which we'll do later in this workbook, but you've now written a query letter! Next, we'll cover some special cases for various other types of projects.

OTHER TYPES OF QUERIES

If you're not writing a fiction or memoir query, you've come to the right section. Here, I'll talk about picture book/graphic novel and nonfiction queries, as those broad categories require a slightly different approach.

NONFICTION QUERIES

You've likely heard that nonfiction projects are sold on proposal. (Specifically, nonfiction for adult readers. For nonfiction picture books, see the following page.)

For nonfiction pitches, the query letter and its attendant proposal identify or create a sense of market need for your specific slant on a topic. Writing an entire book proposal is beyond the scope of this workbook, but I'd strongly recommend *The Weekend Book Proposal* by Ryan Van Cleave (Writer's Digest Books/Penguin Random House).

The query's goal—if you're pitching nonfiction on proposal—is simply to have a gatekeeper request the proposal and sample chapters. Stimulate the idea that the market *needs* this project, with *this* slant, for *this* target audience, written by *this* specific author with *these* specific credentials.

Book proposal queries (which are more cover letters than anything else) will focus on the market, the unique selling proposition of the project, and your marketing reach within the potential target audience.

PICTURE BOOK QUERIES

Fiction picture book queries will focus on character, plot, and the universal theme or lesson learned, similar to the fiction and memoir queries described in the previous section. Nonfiction picture book queries will focus on sales hooks and potential school curriculum tie-ins, since schools and libraries are the primary customers for these types of books. Picture book manuscripts (both fiction and nonfiction) will usually be enclosed after the pitch in their entirety, so the query that presents them can be shorter. (For more on all aspects of picture books, see my book, *Writing Irresistible Picture Books*.)

ILLUSTRATED PROJECT QUERIES

This section will mostly refer to picture book projects that are being pitched *with* illustrations, but I acknowledge that other kinds of books have visual or design elements that their creators will want considered alongside the text. If you're planning to illustrate your book project, or have hired someone to provide visual assets, you should have the following components ready before submission:

- the query letter;
- a copy of the picture book text or graphic novel script as a standalone manuscript file;
- if yours is a traditional picture book, a "sketch dummy" of the full picture book with two or three "mock finishes"; or
- if yours is a graphic novel or manga, include a series of sketches and finishes from one or two sample chapters.

Do you "have to" illustrate a picture book or hire an illustrator before submission? No. Publishers like to select illustrators—and will pay for the art.

Commissioning illustrations can be very expensive, especially if you want something that looks good. For graphic novels and other illustrated projects, you are expected to provide several chapters' worth of illustrations with your text submission. You should have the full script complete and ready to send, if requested.

The "sketch dummy" refers to a PDF of the entire picture book or sample graphic novel chapters, paginated and laid out as it would appear in print form. However, the illustrations are not finished, which lets the creator submit without taking the time to finish each spread. This is strategic, as revisions might be suggested down the road, and the illustrations will have to be redone. Loose black and white pencil or other sketches are fine here.

PDF is the most popular format for graphic dummies, while individual images can be formatted as .jpg, .jpeg, or .png files. The term "mock finishes" refers to two or three pages of the dummy which get the full color "finished" treatment. The dummy should also include the text overlaid or otherwise laid out on the pages. For any project with a visual component, your submission package would not be considered complete without your intended illustrations.

But this is where many artists and designers run into a big problem. How do you transmit your dummy and/or images without sending an unsolicited attachment? (Most submission guidelines prohibit attachments, even if you're clever enough to find an agent's direct, non-query email address. Do not do this. Always follow guidelines and contact gatekeepers how they want to be contacted.)

The solution is to host your work online. But take heart, I don't mean that you should post it widely for (potentially) all to see, especially if you feel protective over your idea. Instead, I recommend hosting the relevant files on your website and then either sending around a download link, or putting them on a page that's password protected and sending a direct link and login credentials in the query. If you do this, you can limit public exposure.

You can also upload files to Google Drive, Dropbox, iCloud, WeTransfer, or a similar cloud-based document storage service and send a direct download link in the query. Note that some of these services have file size limits (picture book dummies tend to be big files) or download expiration dates.

If your file link expires after a week, an agent will likely miss that timeframe, so be extra sure that you're aware of any restrictions to the upload/download process. I'd personally reconsider sending any link that expires, period. Make it easy for the agent or publisher to evaluate you, and erase all potential barriers. If the link is broken, they can't access the file, the permissions are invalid, etc., the gatekeeper might decide that your project isn't worth the hassle.

If you're an aspiring illustrator or author-illustrator, think beyond the project-specific dummy. You should also put up an online portfolio with at least five sample images that reflect all of your different styles and talents. Consider rounding out your portfolio with some characters, scenes, as well as full bleed spreads and spot illustrations. While you may want to keep a specific dummy private, a general portfolio should be widely available for viewing, especially if you're going to be directing agents and art directors to your website.

This rounds out our consideration of special query letter types. Now ... you try it! If you're not writing a nonfiction or picture book project, respectively, you can use the following worksheets to keep refining your fiction or memoir query!

BUILD YOUR NONFICTION QUERY LETTER

See the fiction query worksheet for full
descriptions of each section.

PERSONALIZATION*:

For example: "I'm querying you because you represented my favorite book, *Title*."

COMPARATIVE TITLES*:

1

2

3

LOGLINE*:

*These elements are optional,
but may help you stand out in the slush pile.

MANUSCRIPT LOGISTICS:

The title and word count are the bare minimum here.
For example: "TITLE is a groundbreaking business thought leadership guide, proposed to be 80,000 words."

THE QUERY MEAT:

- Why does the world need this book now, and why are you the expert to write it?
- Read the backs of published books and their sales page marketing copy. This is roughly the length and tone you're going for.
- Keep your query letter to 300 words, or up to one single-spaced page. If you're beyond 400 words, this is unusual (and likely unnecessary), since a nonfiction query often repeats and summarizes data that will be in your book proposal document.
- Write it out on the following pages:

THE QUERY MEAT (CONT.):

BIOGRAPHICAL INFO:

Don't make your bio longer than the query meat. Include only professional-sounding and relevant details. Make sure to cite your publication or contest names and years, if relevant. Italicize book, journal, and periodical titles. For nonfiction, especially, this is the time to brag!

QUERY LOGISTICS:

It can literally be: *Per your guidelines, the proposal and two sample chapters are available upon request. Please note that this is a simultaneous submission. Thank you very much for your time and consideration.*

NAME AND SIGNATURE:

Your real name:

Your pen name (if you're using one):

Best contact info (email and phone number):

Website URLs or social media profiles (feel free to emphasize follower counts and subscribers, if they're noteworthy):

BUILD YOUR PICTURE BOOK QUERY LETTER

See the fiction query worksheet for full
descriptions of each section.

PERSONALIZATION*:

For example: "I'm querying you because you represented my favorite book, *Title*."

COMPARATIVE TITLES*:

1	
2	
3	

LOGLINE*:

*These elements are optional,
but may help you stand out in the slush pile.

MANUSCRIPT LOGISTICS:

The title and word count are the bare minimum here.
For example: "TITLE is a 600-word bedtime book told in rollicking rhyme."

THE QUERY MEAT:

- Give your fiction picture book the full query meat treatment, per the previous section. For a nonfiction picture book, focus on curriculum tie-in opportunities that might make it a strong seller in schools.
- Nonfiction picture books are evergreen, so make sure you do your comp title research. If your topic has already been heavily represented in the market, try to find a fresh angle.
- Read the backs of published books and their sales page marketing copy. This is roughly the length and tone you're going for.
- Keep your query letter to 300 words, or up to one single-spaced page. If you're beyond 400 words, this is unusual (and likely unnecessary).
- Write it out on the following pages.

THE QUERY MEAT (CONT.):

BIOGRAPHICAL INFO:

Don't make your bio longer than the query meat. Include only professional-sounding and relevant details. Make sure to cite your publication or contest names and years, if relevant. Italicize book, journal, and periodical titles.

QUERY LOGISTICS:

This is your breezy sign-off to the query letter itself.

It can literally be: *Per your guidelines, the complete manuscript is pasted below. Please note that this is a simultaneous submission. Thank you very much for your time and consideration.*

NAME AND SIGNATURE:

Don't overcomplicate it, and don't hide your true identity,
even if you choose to use a pen name.

Your real name:

Your pen name (if you're using one):

Best contact info (email and phone number):

Website URLs or social media profiles:

QUERY LETTER FORMATTING

In the previous sections, I presented the basic query elements as separate ingredients. Now, we will combine them into a formatted query letter. It's true that you can hit these points in your preferred order and there isn't just one way to do it. I'm recommending three options for organizing these components—but mine are not the only three options available. Remember that a few elements (like personalization and logline) are optional.

The more information you can include about your project right away (and the more correct and relevant it is, given your market knowledge), the better. Keep in mind that most queries are going to run between 200-400 words. A query's absolute maximum length is one single-spaced printed page with standard 1" margins all around.

PRO TIP: You'll see me say "paragraph" on the following pages, but I mean individual sections of the query, which may only contain a line or two of material. If you find you have a lot of short paragraphs, you are welcome to combine them.

Here are some options for arranging your query components into a polished letter:

EXAMPLE QUERY #1:

- PARAGRAPH 1: Personalization
- PARAGRAPH 2: Logline, Comps, Manuscript Logistics
- PARAGRAPHS 3-5: Query Meat
- PARAGRAPH 6: Bio Info
- PARAGRAPH 7: Query Logistics
- Signature

EXAMPLE QUERY #2:

- PARAGRAPH 1: Manuscript Logistics and Comps
- PARAGRAPHS 2-3: Query Meat
- PARAGRAPH 4: Bio Info
- PARAGRAPH 5: Query Logistics
- Signature

EXAMPLE QUERY #3:

- PARAGRAPHS 1-3: Query Meat
- PARAGRAPH 4: Bio Info
- PARAGRAPH 5: Personalization and Manuscript Logistics
- PARAGRAPH 6: Query Logistics
- Signature

Any manuscript material that you're planning on including will go after the signature portion. As you'll see later in the submission best practices section of this workbook, you will likely end up copying and pasting your material.

ADDRESSING THE QUERY

Most queries (99% of them) are sent and received via email or submission form these days, so you won't find any outdated advice about SASEs here!

In fact, you can completely skip some old-fashioned elements, like the date, recipient mailing address, and sender mailing address at the top of the query. This is a letter writing convention that doesn't play in email.

Simply start with "Dear …" on the first line. Always use a name, unless you simply cannot find one (a publisher who asks you to target your pitch to the "Submissions Editor" is an example). Depending on your research into agents and publishers, you can decide how formal to be. I'd avoid addressing an agent or editor simply by their first name, but Jane Doe or Ms. Doe are good options. ("Dear Sir" is a bit tone-deaf, since a lot of publishing professionals are women.) **Please avoid "To Whom It May Concern."**

SPACING AND FORMATTING

Queries are traditionally single-spaced. To be email-friendly, they don't use indented first lines. Your best bet is to left-justify everything and use a line break between paragraphs.

Copying and pasting is the gold standard, since most agents and publishers do not accept attachments. Note that copying and pasting from a word processor into email can wreak havoc on formatting, including line spacing and indents. Try it and see what happens. Send an email to yourself first to test how your formatting looks on the receiving end. If the results make you happy, then copy and paste your materials from this test email into fresh email messages when you're ready to submit.

Copying and pasting from email to email tends to be more foolproof than going from a word processor into email. If your experiment was a misfire, play around with creating the text in an email compose window.

Agency and publisher submission guidelines differ, but many gatekeepers ask for ten pages or three chapters for a novel or memoir as the writing sample. This generally refers to the beginning of the story and includes the prologue, if you have one.

Do not send a random snippet from the middle of the book, even if "that's where it gets really good." Writing a novel or memoir opening is very hard (*that* is another book entirely!). Don't try to weasel out of exposing your slow or backstory-dense beginning by sending a snapshot of your climax instead. If you find your beginning needs some pep, focus on revision before submission. This is a story issue, not a query one.

TIME TO WRITE!

Take another stab at your query letter, just to get the structure in your bones. No peeking back to the ingredients. Try to remember them!

_____

_____

_____

_____

_____

_____

_____

_____

_____

_____

_____

_____

_____

THE SYNOPSIS

Many writers hate creating a synopsis—and for good reason. This document tends to be dry, full of facts, and dull to read. As writers, we always want to add voice to our work. This is nearly impossible in a synopsis. Here's a dirty synopsis secret: If you hate writing it, they will probably hate reading it just as much. You'll notice that some agents don't even ask for a synopsis. This is good news. The pressure is off!

Alas, I would still recommend preparing one, in case someone requests it as part of the submission package or alongside a partial or full manuscript. Just do your best to convey the flow of your story, and you likely won't be evaluated too harshly on this document alone. Here are some synopsis considerations to keep in mind:

- The synopsis should be two double-spaced pages, though some agents request one single-spaced page (believe it or not, this is not the same amount of text). I'd suggest doing an exercise and writing two versions, one short, one longer (up to three double-spaced pages).
- Your synopsis should contain a chronological retelling of your plot, alongside big-deal character developments, and relevant world-building details.
- Yes, you do need to reveal any plot twists or surprise endings. Agents and publishers will want to see the full scope of your plot.
- The tone of the synopsis should be very matter-of-fact. This is not a document where you should pitch, tease, or withhold information.

- If the synopsis feels dry, that's because it is. The query usually has some sizzle, but synopsis expectations are different, and that's okay!
- If you find yourself with an overlong synopsis, think of all the things you could delete that, if missing, wouldn't impact the reader's understanding of the core story.
- Clarity is key, above all else. The synopsis should present information, not raise questions or introduce confusion.
- Give your synopsis to a friend or critique partner. Then ask your reader to tell you the gist of your story. If they seem totally confused, it's time to take a second look at your document, or throw it away and start all over again. (Sometimes the nuclear option is the most effective.)
- Now knock it out, worry a bit less, and you'll be on your way!

TIME TO WRITE!

Try out a synopsis draft, just to get it down on paper.

_____

_____

_____

_____

_____

_____

_____

_____

_____

QUERY VOICE AND WRITING STYLE

Think of book marketing copy (back, flap, or web description) when writing your query. Aim for voice but don't make it too gimmicky or over the top—humor can be risky unless it fits with your overall book's style. For example, you can crack jokes in a pitch for a humorous midlife crisis essay collection, but the same approach would be less appropriate in a thought leadership nonfiction pitch (unless you're an anti-corporate-culture warrior, for example).

The most important thing to know is that queries and synopses are read **VERY QUICKLY**. Nobody likes to hear this, but queries are scanned like items on a belt at the grocery store. A gatekeeper is sitting down to read maybe 200 to 300 submissions at a time (because they'll receive 10,000 or more per year, and they generally don't have time to read slush ever day).

Acquisitions editors at publishing houses likely receive fewer submissions, unless that publisher is open to unagented projects, and will take more time with their reading. Still, a lot of the principles here apply to their decision process as well.

What this means for you: Be brief, be clear, be intentional. Don't over-indulge in long sentences or complex syntax. If you run out of breath reading a sentence from your query aloud—yes, you should absolutely do this—then that sentence is too long or nuanced. Make your work scannable. Make it legible. Make it a joy to breeze through.

In terms of tone, you will ideally come across as confident but not boastful or cocky. (This goes for your writing style as well as what you talk about, like getting ahead of yourself and pitching potential Oscar-winning actors who would *obviously* love to star in the movie version ... before the book even exists. See page 130 for more on that.)

I'd strongly examine each and every adjective in the query, especially those applied to your work or yourself. Ideally, you have a certain measure of belief in yourself and think the project is strong. You wrote it! However, no kind of self-judgment (good or bad) belongs in your query letter.

In the specificity exercise on page 25, I referenced Dave Eggers's *A Heartbreaking Work of Staggering Genius*. This title is used ironically and fits the author's style. You better not show up in the slush pile calling your own project "a heartbreaking work of staggering genius" in earnest.

This goes for comparing yourself to obvious bestsellers. (In the heyday of fantasy and paranormal MG and YA, my slush pile was full of writers claiming to be "*Harry Potter* meets *Twilight*." My optometrist is still working on retrieving my eyeballs from the back of my head.)

Agents and publishers are obviously screening you for your project, hook, and ability to write. But they're *also* screening you for a sense of how pleasurable you'd be to work with. This includes easy confidence and humility, not boastful delusions of grandeur. (And unrealistic expectations.)

A similar note—but given more gently—applies to assertions like "this is my debut novel" and "I'm pre-published." I completely understand the good intentions behind these phrases, but they can come across as amateur.

VOICE & WRITING STYLE CHECKLIST

01 My query and synopsis are simple, succinct, and easy to read. YES ☐ NO ☐

02 It's fun to scan my shorter sentences, especially for someone reading 300 queries in one sitting. YES ☐ NO ☐

03 I exclude unnecessary details and flourishes and don't use overly complex syntax. YES ☐ NO ☐

04 If I attempt humor or voice, it aligns with my project's tone and topic. YES ☐ NO ☐

05 I've been reading my work aloud as I compose it, so I know it flows well. YES ☐ NO ☐

06 Even better, I've had someone else read my query aloud to me. I've noted where they stumble or flub words. YES ☐ NO ☐

07 I come across as competent and professional with just enough personality. YES ☐ NO ☐

08 My query is free of boasting and superfluous adjectives about myself and my own work. YES ☐ NO ☐

MANUSCRIPT FORMATTING

Once your query does its job, you'll be asked for a full or partial manuscript. When that happens, you should be able to show them a professional-looking document. Manuscript formatting tends to confuse a lot of writers, but it doesn't need to be intimidating.

Remember that you will likely be initially submitting your manuscript copied and pasted into an email or submission form, so a lot of your intentional formatting might be lost during the evaluation phase. Don't expect everything to look like a perfect approximation of your Word document. That said, I strongly encourage all aspiring writers to follow industry-standard formatting guidelines anyway.

Presenting your manuscript professionally from the very beginning, even if you're the only person looking at it, sets a polished tone for the entire creation experience and makes potential future submissions easier.

MANUSCRIPT FORMATTING

Here's an example of proper manuscript formatting. This information should be on a separate cover page:

Mary Kole
123 Main St.
Town, State, ZIP
(212) 555-5555
mary@goodstorycompany.com

Bolded Manuscript Title
By Mary Kole
Genre/Category
# of words

Now here's a manuscript page, and I've included a line that's meant to represent a header at the top (this can also go on the bottom). Add a few new lines, then start with a chapter heading (for fiction and memoir):

Manuscript Title / Kole / Page #

Chapter 1

You don't have to indent your first line, but do intent future lines to an

industry-standard .5". Use double-spacing, 12-point font, such as Times

New Roman, and 1" margins all around!

 "Let's start a new line," Mary said.

MANUSCRIPT FORMATTING CHECKLIST

01 — My margins are 1" all around, with indents going out to .5" for each new line of prose, except the first line of a chapter. YES ☐ NO ☐

02 — I've used a 12-point font, like Times New Roman. YES ☐ NO ☐

03 — **I've begrudgingly accepted that my formatting won't carry over to email or form submissions.** YES ☐ NO ☐

04 — But I'm committing to properly formatting the document for my own dignity anyway! YES ☐ NO ☐

05 — While I know not to include this when copying and pasting my sample, my document has a cover page which features the: YES ☐ NO ☐
- Title
- Byline
- Word count
- Contact information/socials

06 — If I'm using a header, I've included the following: YES ☐ NO ☐
- Manuscript title
- Last name
- Total number of pages

REVISING YOUR QUERY

Writing a query for the first time is hard. It can be discombobulating to distill your entire life's work into 400 words, especially for the first time. Plus, pitching and query-writing differ from creative writing, so you're honing unique skills and being asked to learn a new type of written communication.

The good news is, revising a query is much easier once the draft of the darn thing exists. Read it aloud to yourself, then give it to someone who isn't familiar with your story and ask them to tell the gist back to you (as they understand it). This can mean the main story, for fiction and memoir, or the main sales hooks, for nonfiction. You won't be able to stand over the gatekeeper's shoulder and explain or contextualize when the query lands in their slush pile, so you can't buttress your query with explanation when someone else reviews it. The document must speak for itself.

You should also finalize the substance of the query before you start worrying about revising the writing style and voice. (You'll notice that the writing checklist features much later in this section than your character and plot revision checklists. This is on purpose.) Before you mess with the language, you need to make sure that the query gets the relevant information across.

Use the following pages to make sure you're on track!

MARKET TARGETING CHECKLIST

		YES	NO
01	My project fits an established category and genre.	☐	☐
02	My word count is within a normal range (see pages 18 and 19.)	☐	☐
03	I've figured out at least three comparative titles that fit comp title criteria and address the same target audience and genre (for the most part).	☐	☐
04	If I use any unique narrative choices (multiple POVs, an interesting chronology), I mention that in the manuscript logistics part of the query.	☐	☐
05	This VERY IMPORTANT data (personalization, comps, title, word count, genre, audience) appears at the very top of the query.	☐	☐
06	I understand my category and genre tropes and expectations, and I'm either brilliantly playing with them or cleverly subverting them.	☐	☐
07	My manuscript or proposal is well formatted and ready to go in case someone requests it, which is the whole point of the query letter!	☐	☐

QUERY PREMISE CHECKLIST

01 My project has a clear theme or mission statement which positively impacts its marketability/timeliness, though I don't dwell on it much in the query itself.

YES ☐ NO ☐

My book's theme or the project's mission statement is:

02 My query asks a dramatic question (for narrative projects) and comes back full circle to answering or escalating that question at the end.

YES ☐ NO ☐

03 Every detail in the query is chosen to either spotlight character, advance plot, showcase world, fit the theme, or serve the dramatic question.

YES ☐ NO ☐

04 I understand that if a detail is too granular or doesn't serve a reader's big-picture understanding of the query, I should let it go. Same for information that's redundant (multiple meditations on the theme, for example).

YES ☐ NO ☐

05 I avoid philosophizing about the target audience (e.g., "Women at midlife tend to read strong female protagonists," etc.), even in my bio, where I might be tempted to explain why I wrote the project. (Discussion of theme and audience is more appropriate in memoir and nonfiction.)

YES ☐   NO ☐

06 To that end, I also limit my discussion of why I wrote the project (unless it's relevant to the sales hook of the memoir or nonfiction work) and my inspiration. This feels very important to you but might not be relevant at the query stage.

YES ☐   NO ☐

07 I've rewritten my logline statement, and I'll express it here:

YES ☐   NO ☐

---

08 I've settled on three comparative titles to use in the query, ideally published within the last three years:

YES ☐　NO ☐

Three comparative titles—that share elements in common with my project, but are different enough from it that mine stands out—are:
1
2
3

09 At the same time, my project is distinct enough from them in the following ways:

YES ☐　NO ☐

CHARACTER REVISION CHECKLIST

01 My main character is described in a proactive way and leads the plot as much as possible in the query.

YES ☐ NO ☐

02 I've mentioned up to three supporting characters, but they absolutely have to be in the query because they have clear conflicts with the protagonist.

YES ☐ NO ☐

03 If I'm using multiple POVs, each has a clear intersection point with the plot and other characters.

YES ☐ NO ☐

04 The main character is featured at the beginning, middle, and end of the query.

YES ☐ NO ☐

05 Their growth arc is alluded to or the query charts a strong sense of change or forward momentum for my protagonist.

YES ☐ NO ☐

06 Readers are inspired to care about the character because they know their objective, motivation, or need.

YES ☐ NO ☐

07 There is a reason for their want and need, and this can be hinted at.

YES ☐ NO ☐

| 08 | There's a sense of stakes, or of why this particular character's need or desire matters to them. | YES ☐ | NO ☐ |

| 09 | If I stray from this format, there's a good reason to include other details. | YES ☐ | NO ☐ |

| 10 | The resolution speaks to the character's growth and development arc, even if we don't overtly focus on theme. | YES ☐ | NO ☐ |

MEMOIR WRITERS:

It can be awkward to consider a memoir "character" as a separate entity because **you are the protagonist**. But you are showcasing an edited version of yourself in a memoir, just as you are showcasing an edited version of your life story (it's impossible to include everything, after all). To this end, make sure you're pitching your transformation, journey, growth, and the takeaways that will most likely speak to your target audience when you define the "protagonist" of your memoir. A lot of fiction conventions apply to narrative nonfiction.

The following revision checklists tackle plot and structure, which doesn't generally get a ton of detail in the query, but you should make sure to hit some important points.

PLOT REVISION CHECKLIST

01

What type of conflict does your narrative feature?

- [ ] Character vs. other character/antagonist
- [ ] Character vs. society
- [ ] Character vs. larger world antagonist
- [ ] Character vs. betrayal
- [ ] Character vs. self
- [ ] Character vs. their past

02

Is your conflict **acute** or **chronic** (new or ongoing)?

- [ ] Acute
- [ ] Chronic

03

Is your conflict **internal** or **external**?
(The character grapples within themselves OR with an event or situation that acts upon them from the outside.)

- [ ] Internal
- [ ] External
- [ ] Both

04

There's a clear reason why the story starts **today**, as opposed to yesterday or next week (remember your inciting incident).

YES [ ]   NO [ ]

05 The events of the story flow in a cause-and-effect sequence, rather than happening seemingly randomly. This progression is clear in the query.

YES ☐   NO ☐

---

06 The beginning of the query seems to circle back to the end or refer to the opening conflict in some way. (If the query takes a left turn without referring back to the opening conflict, this might seem jarring or incongruent.)

YES ☐   NO ☐

---

07 My query has a good balance of:

YES ☐   NO ☐

☐ Character description

☐ Objective/motivation

☐ Antagonism/obstacles

☐ Sense of stakes

☐ Deeper impact on character

MEMOIR AND NONFICTION WRITERS:

Most of these query revision checklists have referred to fiction projects. However, many of these ideas can apply to memoirs (and narrative nonfiction). How can you incorporate storytelling ideas into your memoir or nonfiction project?

Nonfiction writers can create an ideal customer avatar and throw the problem your book solves at them, so you can also consider obstacles, stakes, and conflict. Your nonfiction book should address a common issue or help people, so consider applying these concepts to the need or problem that your audience has.

STRUCTURE REVISION CHECKLIST

01 My story has a definite beginning, middle, and end.

YES ☐   NO ☐

02 There is conflict introduced in the first paragraph.

YES ☐   NO ☐

03 Characters have tension or conflict with one another, rather than simply coexisting. This conflict drives the story forward.

YES ☐   NO ☐

04 My story has both internal and external conflict.

YES ☐   NO ☐

05 The story incorporates stakes, or a reason why the story matters to the character (and therefore the reader).

YES ☐   NO ☐

06 The initial conflict either escalates throughout, or the conflict transforms or transitions around the midpoint.

YES ☐   NO ☐

07 The story has an engaging resolution that's hinted at in the query, or outright expressed to showcase your plotting prowess. (Don't fear revealing the end!)

YES ☐   NO ☐

QUERY WORLD-BUILDING WORKSHEET

What are the unique elements of your speculative or historical world (if applicable) that make your book stand out?

How do you describe them in the query?

How do these elements directly impact the main character?

How do these elements directly impact the plot?

What's the logic of why the magic/society works as it does?

SENTENCE-LEVEL REVISION CHECKLIST

01 I've read my work aloud. — YES ☐ NO ☐

02 Someone has read my work aloud to me. — YES ☐ NO ☐

03 I've actually done both of the above instead of sitting there, thinking it's a good idea, and then not doing it. — YES ☐ NO ☐

04 My sentences are **short** and **scannable**. — YES ☐ NO ☐

05 I've worked hard to write clearly, rather than indulging in formal phrasing or unnecessary wordiness. — YES ☐ NO ☐

06 My sentence syntax is not complex or confusing. — YES ☐ NO ☐

07 There are no adjectives, boastful claims, or thematic meditations cluttering up the query. — YES ☐ NO ☐

08 My tone and voice are professional unless there's an obvious reason to use humor and get chatty (even then, try to rein it in). — YES ☐ NO ☐

GETTING
FEEDBACK

Outside feedback is important because, while you know what you're doing (you hope), you need to make sure it tracks with a third party. Especially when it comes to a query letter, where the imbalance of information is so dire. You know the **entire** story, the reader knows **nothing**. A lot is expected of you in a short amount of time (which is why some writers really dislike the perceived pressure of the query letter). It's always good to put your query to the test with someone else. This advice has been mentioned several times throughout this workbook, but now it's time to examine it more closely.

When you give your pitch to someone who doesn't know it, that's the real test of whether it's ready for an audience. However, this other person should be qualified to give you constructive feedback. You don't want to give your manuscript to any random person off the street and, counterintuitively, you don't want to give it to a loved one, either

Random laypeople and loved ones aren't good at commenting on query letters because the query is such a specific document, full of industry conventions. You also have to consider your relationship to the person you're seeking feedback from. Randos are unlikely to care and loved ones will (hopefully) praise whatever you're doing, even if they don't understand it.

Also, feedback like "It's good!" doesn't actually tell you anything, even if it feels temporarily nice. Most people you might find who'll read your query (and synopsis) won't have the critical understanding or language to go beyond broad value judgments.

I work as a freelance editor—I make my living when writers show up to ask me for feedback on their projects, including their queries (the Query and Synopsis Edit and the Submission Package Edit are two of my most popular services).

That makes me biased, because I have a vested financial interest in recommending that you get outside feedback. But I am plenty busy, and that's not why I'm giving this advice. **If you don't want to pay for feedback, it's very possible to cultivate critique relationships for free.** (As long as the writers who will be evaluating your work know something about query letters, and especially your specific genre and category. Otherwise their advice is not going to be that fruitful.)

The best person to give you query letter feedback is either an adult who has read a lot of query letters, another writer who specializes in your specific segment of the market, or a paid professional editor who knows your genre and target audience well. Personal experience with pitches—such as previous or current work as an agent or acquisitions editor—is also a bonus.

NEXT STEPS: GETTING FEEDBACK

			YES	NO
01	I've gotten feedback about my project from at least one outside source.		☐	☐
02	If desired, I've gotten feedback from a freelance editor who specializes in queries.		☐	☐
03	I've made revisions to my story based on outside feedback, focusing on the clarity with which my core idea is communicated.		☐	☐
04	I've gone back through the revision checklists in the previous section to make sure all the elements of my story are clicking.		☐	☐
05	I've set my query aside for **at least two weeks** to come back with fresh eyes.		☐	☐

WHEN IS IT DONE?

You might never be fully satisfied with your project *or* your submission materials. That's normal. Even multi-published writers wish they could change books that are already on shelves. When you've exhausted your revision energy and find yourself moving commas around, it might be time for next steps.

And that means ...

SUBMISSION!

SUBMISSION BEST PRACTICES

At long last, let's discuss the logistics of submitting to literary agents and publishers, submission strategies, research resources, and more.

You will ideally be submitting your project when it's the strongest you can possibly get it, after revising it and putting it away for a few weeks for one last dose of clarity (this also goes for your query, per the previous section).

At this point, you might be thinking about your overall "author brand," and how you will come across to gatekeepers. Consider whether there's a thematic or stylistic element that pulls together the stories you want to tell. Do you want to work in more than one category or with more than one genre? Are there any common threads? (Most gatekeepers will suggest that you publish two projects in the same category or genre first, before branching out. This will allow you to build a readership more effectively. Make sure you query agents who represent all of your desired niches, if you're interested in writing more than one type of book.)

If you've done the work and used all of the principles in this workbook, then there might well be someone out there who's eager for your query. This is your opportunity to put your submission package together and get out into the world!

If you're on the fence about whether to self-publish or go the traditional route, you won't lose anything by trying one or two submission rounds to agents and publishers. While self-publishing a book is beyond the scope of this guide, you need to know that independent publishing hinges on the author's marketing ability. If that doesn't sound appealing, you have some choices to make!

In the following pages, you'll get submission research resources to help you find literary agents and publishers who take submissions directly from writers. You should then go and research each target's submission guidelines (usually listed on their websites). These can often be reprinted elsewhere but may not be current in a third-party database, so go right to the source.

Once you know what each target wants to see from you (and you've confirmed that they're still at their agency or publisher and open to submissions), you will do one last quality check and send your materials. (It can be a big bummer, but agents often close to submissions due to overwhelm or events in their personal lives, and you might not learn this until "go time." This is why you will ideally have a number of names to choose from.)

I strongly suggest researching about 30 individual names and submitting in rounds to 10-15 gatekeepers at a time (see the following pages for exact details). This will allow you to gauge responses and redirect your pitch or project, if necessary.

Pay close attention to this phase of the process, as it's where a lot of preventable mistakes are made. You've spent months or years on your book. Give the query and submission period of your writing life the same care and consideration.

Before we dive into the nitty gritty, you mind find it helpful to see a 30,000-foot overview of the entire submission process. After all, the more you know, the more prepared you can be.

SUBMISSION STRATEGY

I'll summarize the submission process here, with a rehash of the pre-submission steps for good measure:

1. Write the very best manuscript you can, with an eye toward the market for your potential idea. The biggest mistakes are made at this point, especially if you aren't yet intentional about what you're writing or who you're writing it for.
2. Bring all of your writing craft knowledge to bear on a killer revision of said manuscript. Writers are notoriously bad at seeing issues with their own work, so it's best to involve a second set of eyes, whether a critique partner, writing group, beta reader, or freelance editor.
3. Revise, like, ten more times.
4. Get very, very sick of your project.
5. Put it aside for a month. (No, seriously!)
6. Revise one last time!
7. Agonize over the query letter and synopsis as you put your submission package together.
8. Stare at the wall and reconsider all of the life choices that led you to this point.
9. Do solid agent and publisher research and make your "A List" and "B List." **A lot of mistakes are made at this point, especially as anticipation and impatience assert themselves**.
10. Compile everyone's submission guidelines.
11. Ride a bizarre emotional rollercoaster, convinced you're either a genius or a hack. Or sometimes both, all within the same moment.
12. Put together your submissions, paying attention to individual submission guidelines and formatting (to the best of your ability).
13. Press "Send" on your emails and forms!
14. Hear back, usually over the course of weeks or months. You should have all the responses you're going to get after four months.

117

15. See step 8 on the previous page.

16. Scrape together the feedback you've gotten. (A complete lack of personalized feedback is also feedback, in and of itself.) See if you can spot any patterns.

17. Make a revision plan or decide to "take the wisdom and leave the rest" from this particular project and put it away, either temporarily or permanently.

18. Either enact your revision plan or work on something new.

19. See step 8 again.

20. If you're sticking with the project, put together your next submission round, calling on your "B List" and any targets from your "A List" who seemed promising.

21. Don't forget to come up for air, read for pleasure, talk to humans, and do some self-care. (If you figure out this whole work-life balance thing, let me know.)

You might be very discouraged to read about all of the revision you might end up doing. Get used to it, though! If you land an agent, you'll likely revise again. A book deal? More revision. You'd do well to learn to love it ASAP because revision isn't going anywhere.

Next, let's revisit your submission goals.

SUBMISSION GOALS QUESTIONNAIRE

01 Now that you've gone through the query writing and revision process, revisit your primary publishing goal for this project. What do you want this to accomplish for you?

> Try to be more specific than "get published."

02 What is the exact audience you're envisioning for this project?

03 How confident do you feel about having a potential place in the market, as it exists now, for your type of book?

How much help and guidance do you want from a potential agent or publisher?

04

☐ Communicate with them often

☐ Be left to your own devices

---

05 How much control and input do you want during the publication process? (Your answer here might point you firmly toward either traditional or self-publishing.)

What size of agency or publisher feels right to you?

06

☐ Large corporation with many clients/authors

☐ A cozy boutique with smaller lists and more individual attention (though size doesn't always reflect attentiveness)

---

07 What kind of peers do you envision surrounding yourself with? Do you care about the other authors at that agency or house?

08 How many projects do you have in you as a writer? How often do you imagine coming up with a book that's ready for publication?

> There is no right or wrong answer here, but having too many projects that you'd like to publish all at once—as some creators do—can actually be a liability, as very few houses will do more than one book every year or two.

09 How important is money?

☐ Very   ☐ Somewhat   ☐ Not important

10 How important are subrights (movie, merchandising, audio, foreign, etc.)?

☐ Very   ☐ Somewhat   ☐ Not important

11 Are you more comfortable with ...

☐ An advance

☐ A royalty-only deal (happens with some small publishers)

☐ A combination of the above

SUBMISSION RESOURCES

Below, you'll find a list of submission resources that you can use to research your targets. Many writers use some or all of these to weave together a solid sense of who's out there in the publishing world, and what their tastes might be. **Take your time with this research!**

Manuscript Wish List

- manuscriptwishlist.com and the #mswl hashtag
  - A great and frequently updated resource that collects "wish list" mentions from agents and acquiring editors.

Association of American Literary Agents

- aalitagents.org
  - A list of member agencies that have agreed to abide by certain ethics codes and standards.

Literary Rambles

- literaryrambles.com
  - A roundup of agent interviews, web presence, and submission information. Learn more about various agents here. This resource sometimes spotlights new agents on the scene.

Agent Query

- agentquery.com
  - A searchable database of agents that you can sort by category and genre.

Bitsy Kemper

- https://bitsykemper.com/publishers/
  - A list of children's book publishers (specifically) that don't require an agent.

Writer's Digest

- writersdigest.com
  - A great resource for writers, with profiles of agents, interviews with authors about their agents or publishers, and insight into the ins and outs of the industry.

Writer's Market

- Book from Writer's Digest Books/Penguin Random House
  - A regularly updated guide (available in print and digital editions) that lists the industry's submission targets, including publishers who accept projects directly. There are separate resources issued for poets and children's creators, as well.

Query Tracker

- querytracker.com
  - Research, organize, and track your submissions.

Duotrope

- duotrope.com
  - A paid submission tracker and resource for finding agents and publishers.

Publishers Marketplace

- publishersmarketplace.com
  - A paid resource for agent and publisher research, as well as a database of book deals and upcoming titles. Includes lists of top dealmakers (agents who have a track record) in many different categories and genres.

Chill Subs

- chillsubs.com
  - A new database of submission opportunities that focuses on small publishers, literary magazines, periodicals, retreats, etc.

BUILD YOUR SUBMISSION STRATEGY

The following pages will help you strategize a submission round to publishers or agents (or both at the same time, which is totally okay). Your first round of research will result in 20- 30 names that seem compelling to you, whether those are publishers that accept unagented submissions or individual literary agents.

#	Agent/Editor	Agency/House	Why They're Interesting
1			
2			
3			
4			
5			
6			
7			
8			
9			
10			
11			

#	Agent/Editor	Agency/House	Why They're Interesting
12			
13			
14			
15			
16			
17			
18			
19			
20			
21			
22			
23			
24			
25			
27			

#	Agent/Editor	Agency/House	Why They're Interesting
28			
29			
30			
31			
32			
33			
34			
35			

THAT'S A LOT OF DATA!

You'll find that you might be surprised by this process. Some of the gatekeepers you found are probably more interesting than you expected, some are less. All seem to be looking for rather vague things, like "literary quality and commercial appeal." (This also happens to agents, who go out to meet acquisitions editors and learn what they want. All acquisition editors seem to say the same thing, and an agent has to infer their desires. But that's part of the job.)

It's impossible to know exactly what an agent or acquisitions editor wants, as everyone has varying tastes in regards not only to concept but to execution as well. However, by using your research resources, you can get close. On the next page, I'll ask you to start sorting your picks.

Now that you know more about each gatekeeper, **segment your targets into an A and a B List of 10-15 names each.** (If you find even more people you'd like to pitch, but are maybe lukewarm about, then you can also create a C List and keep it in your back pocket.)

A LIST	B LIST
1.	1.
2.	2.
3.	3.
4.	4.
5.	5.
6.	6.
7.	7.
8.	8.
9.	9.
10.	10.
11.	11.
12.	12.
13.	13.
14.	14.
15.	15.

C LIST
1.
2.
3.
4.
5.

SUBMISSION DOS AND DON'TS

01 Send to your A List first. That's right. **Go for the brass ring right off the bat.** If someone from your B List offers and you never get to your A List, you will always wonder "What if?"

02 Do not simultaneously pitch more than one editor at a publishing imprint, and more than one agent at a literary agency.

03 It is perfectly acceptable (and beneficial to the writer) to send all your submissions at once (in rounds to your A List first, then your B List). Just make sure to mention that yours is a "simultaneous submission."

04 Do not grant exclusivity (send to one target until they respond, like Early Decision to a college) unless you have a compelling reason to do so (see below).

05 If you are revising for an agent or publisher based on extensive notes they've given you (called a "revise and resubmit"), you should grant them exclusivity to consider the project (for a specified period, like two to four weeks).

06 Do not contact an agent or editor with a revised manuscript unless you have done significant work since submission. If so, you can withdraw your project from consideration and send the new version. **Do not do this more than once (or at all, if you can avoid it).** However, most writers have submitted only to get a great idea for revision and realize they hit "send" too early.

07 Follow all submission guidelines for agents and publishers.

---

08 **Do not send attachments**, unless they are specifically requested.

---

09 Copy and paste your first pages/chapters (or the entire picture book manuscript) after your query in the email or submission form. Don't stress about retaining perfect formatting—they've seen worse.

---

10 **Author/illustrators**: Create a sketch dummy with two or three mock finishes for your project. Host it online on a private page and provide a link. Remember, you shouldn't send attachments or expiring links (see page 64).

---

11 Do keep the entire letter brief and professional, including the bio, which should be short and relevant.

---

12 Do focus on the project at hand. (Don't pitch a handful of projects at a time, but have them ready to discuss, if asked.)

---

13 Don't apologize for or focus on your lack of experience (avoid the term "pre-published", it's aspirational but amateur).

---

14 Avoid vague mentions of contests, publication credits, and awards—be specific if you have legitimate achievements!

---

15 Don't make value judgments about your work—of course you think it's great, you wrote it! If you find adjectives in the query that refer to you or your work, make sure you need them!

16 Do say that a project has "series potential" instead of requiring a series for your story or saying "The first in a trilogy ..." A publisher may not offer a multi-book contract to a debut. (If you absolutely need to sell your idea as a series, then be honest.)

17 Mention only what we absolutely need to know for the story to make sense in the query and synopsis. Don't give too much irrelevant information.

18 Don't state the obvious (eg: "I'm querying you because I want to get published"), be redundant (e.g.: "fiction novel," "picture book for young readers"), or micromanage with useless instructions ("Please use my phone number, below, to call me!"). I've seen these all multiple times in my own slush pile.

19 Focus on the book without discussing ancillary rights (movie and merchandising ideas, etc.). Basically, avoid putting the cart before the horse!
- "Tom Cruise/Hanks would be great in the movie!"

20 Wait six to eight weeks (some agents will specify a response time on their websites). In most cases, if you haven't heard back within this timeframe, that's a no.

21 Notify everyone who has requested your full manuscript or proposal if you receive an offer of representation or a contract from a publisher.

GET AND STAY ORGANIZED!

Every submission round is unique to the writer and project at hand. If you follow these best practices, you will be far ahead of many competing writers in the slush. That said, there's no such thing as a "textbook" submission, even if we can talk about the broad-strokes order of events. The next few steps come into play once you start getting responses (but as we'll see in the following section, not all responses are equal).

Once you've finalized all of the materials you will need for your submission (for fiction, that's the query, synopsis, and completed manuscript with proper formatting; for picture books, that's the query and manuscript, with optional illustrations; and for nonfiction, that's a query and proposal and sample chapters) you can fill out the following tracker spreadsheets for your targets, including their name, where they work, how to contact them (usually an email or submission form), what they want to see (check their submission guidelines), when you sent something to them, and whether you received a response.

In keeping with these best practices, we will start with your A List submission tracker.

A-LIST SUBMISSION TRACKER

#	Agent/Editor	Agency/House	Contact (Email or Form)
1			
2			
3			
4			
5			
6			
7			
8			
9			
10			

A-LIST SUBMISSION TRACKER

#	What to Send?	Sub Date	Response?	Follow-up?
1				
2				
3				
4				
5				
6				
7				
8				
9				
10				

A-LIST SUBMISSION TRACKER

#	Agent/Editor	Agency/House	Contact (Email or Form)
11			
12			
13			
14			
15			
16			
17			
18			
19			
20			

A-LIST SUBMISSION TRACKER

#	What to Send?	Sub Date	Response?	Follow-up?
11				
12				
13				
14				
15				
16				
17				
18				
19				
20				

Once you've put everything together and sent your
submission off into the world, you might feel like a
tree falling in the forest with no one to hear it.

THIS IS NORMAL!

NOW WHAT?

All the excitement of submission can come crashing down when you realize that the process is very "hurry up and wait." Publishing is the slowest industry imaginable, and, unfortunately, this is normal.

Wait up to three months, or until you hear back from everyone who's going to respond to your submission round. If you feel like your message was genuinely overlooked, you can follow up after about six to eight weeks. Sometimes you won't hear back at all, and that's considered a "decline" (a nice industry term for a rejection). Some gatekeepers won't get back to you at all. This is not meant to be disrespectful, but is an unfortunate reality of the business.

Compile the responses you've received. Decide if you have enough new ideas to do a revision, then try resubmitting to a mix of agents who gave you feedback from your A List, as well as some B List and C List targets this time around.

Every submission round is unique. So are the next steps available to you if your query wasn't successful. If you're seeing a wall of "no," did you actually know that there are multiple levels of rejection? Let's unpack what some of your responses mean.

It all depends on whether you got form rejections or actual feedback. The more specific feedback you receive, the more closely your work was considered. Some writers will get a few sentences along the lines of "I didn't connect with the voice" and believe this was personal.

I'm afraid it's usually not, but agents and publishers know that voice is such a nebulous and subjective thing that nobody can really argue with this assessment. A truly personal rejection will mention elements of the story itself, call characters by name, or make revision suggestions that feel targeted to the substance of the project.

If there is actionable feedback in your declines, you might have something concrete to work with. Decide if the notes resonate, and if they do, you can weigh whether you want to revise by yourself or get a critique group or freelance editor to help you.

If you're only getting form rejections, this is a sign that your project simply isn't ready, or that the premise isn't hitting. (I'm including an article about various rejection types in the resource list at the end of this workbook.)

Once you've completed one unsuccessful submission round and a pretty substantial revision of your project, you can try submitting it to the agents on your B List, as well as any agents who you still want to target from your A List (those who sent personal or encouraging declines).

This will be your next submission. I always advocate for smaller submission rounds of ten or fifteen well-targeted names because you never know what kind of feedback you'll get. This allows you to be more responsive to feedback without burning through every available target in one go. Halfway through the process, you might realize that a revision might make you more successful, and if you've held some names in reserve, you'll still have gatekeepers to submit to with a new version.

If you find that you receive a consistent critique of your project, but you've already sent it to every single agent who represents your category, you're a bit SOL. I realize submission is exciting and most writers can't wait to find out what'll happen with their projects. But slow and steady—backed by strong research—often wins the race.

You may notice that I'm seemingly okay with resubmitting to agents who have previously seen—and passed on— the work. Haven't you already blown it with your A List? Not necessarily. In fact, it's perfectly possible to submit to agents who have already rejected you, but only if you can honestly say that you've done a major revision of the project.

Your target initially passed for a reason, whether they expressed that reason to you or not. If you send them the same manuscript with a light revision (moving commas around, mostly), they will probably pass again. But if you've gotten great feedback from your submission round and you've fundamentally revised, you can absolutely try to resubmit.

Be sure to mention in your second query letter that the agent or publisher has seen this project before, but that you've made significant changes. The worst they can do is say "no" once more. This is a low-risk gamble with a lot of potential upside, especially if the agent or publisher offered you some personal feedback the first time around. That means there was some interest there initially that you could try to capitalize on.

Is a "no" from one agent or editor a "no from all" at that agency or publisher, respectively? You will often see this mentioned on an agency or publisher website. It means that a "no" from one person puts the whole company off-limits. For agencies, this may not be true. Most agents maintain their own slush piles, especially if they have a unique, personal email address for slush. (Some agencies and publishers keep generic submission inboxes, though, so this advice doesn't apply.)

If an agent has rejected you and you can be somewhat sure that they're the only person at the agency who saw the work, you can add a different agent from the same company to your B List for the next submission round. It's not an illegal move. For publishers, it's harder to tell because you have no way of knowing who actually reviewed your submission. A resubmission may land in front of the same editor (or intern) who declined it the first time, so sending a project back to a publisher who already passed is more of a gamble.

In the following pages, you'll see a response log, a revision ideas worksheet, and trackers for your B List and C List, if necessary.

FIRST SUBMISSION RESPONSE LOG

Are there any specific or consistent responses you're seeing?
What stands out to you?

_____

_____

_____

_____

_____

_____

_____

_____

_____

_____

_____

_____

_____

POST-SUBMISSION REVISION IDEAS

Do you have any revision ideas post-submission that you'd like to implement??

_____

_____

_____

_____

_____

_____

_____

_____

_____

_____

_____

_____

_____

_____

_____

_____

_____

_____

_____

_____

_____

_____

_____

TAKE A DEEP BREATH...

It may feel vulnerable to go out on submission again, but if you have some revision ideas and more names in your back pocket, you will want to keep trying and use everything you've learned from your previous submission round to get back out there.

On the following pages, list out the names, contact information, and submission guidelines for your B List and potential C List targets. If you resubmit to anyone who has already seen your work, remember to identify yourself as having previously submitted and mention that the project has seen "significant revision" (if true, of course).

B-LIST SUBMISSION TRACKER

#	Agent/Editor	Agency/House	Contact (Email or Form)
1			
2			
3			
4			
5			
6			
7			
8			
9			
10			

B-LIST SUBMISSION TRACKER

#	What to Send?	Sub Date	Response?	Follow-up?
1				
2				
3				
4				
5				
6				
7				
8				
9				
10				

B-LIST SUBMISSION TRACKER

#	Agent/Editor	Agency/House	Contact (Email or Form)
11			
12			
13			
14			
15			
16			
17			
18			
19			
20			

B-LIST SUBMISSION TRACKER

#	What to Send?	Sub Date	Response?	Follow-up?
11				
12				
13				
14				
15				
16				
17				
18				
19				
20				

C-LIST SUBMISSION TRACKER

#	Agent/Editor	Agency/House	Contact (Email or Form)
1			
2			
3			
4			
5			
6			
7			
8			
9			
10			

C-LIST SUBMISSION TRACKER

#	What to Send?	Sub Date	Response?	Follow-up?
1				
2				
3				
4				
5				
6				
7				
8				
9				
10				

STAYING BUSY

Many writers feel that submission "should" be the most active and celebratory part of their writing life to date. And this is true! But you will also want to try and give that validation to yourself, rather than seeking it externally from gatekeepers. Yes, I know—that external validation is sort of *the point* of submission. But the underwhelming truth is that the publishing business is full of rejection, jealousy (have you read *Yellowface* by R.F. Kuang?), and disappointment. (*Not* what you want to hear right now, but I'm going somewhere with this, I swear.) If you've done your best work, you can sit back and let the outcome play out. Sometimes, though, your current best work will not be strong enough for agent representation or a book contract. And that's okay. I promise. Because you can always be learning your craft, honing your skills, and nurturing your artistic self.

If you've submitted to your A List, B List, and C List without success, you'll have to decide whether to scrap the project or revise and try again (though you'll have fewer viable targets). You can also write something new and dust off a shelved project again at a later date, if you decide you want to revisit it. **No time spent writing or submitting is ever wasted. Ever.**

In the meantime, work on your next project, put your current work away and revise it with fresh eyes or based on any feedback you receive, create your online footprint, read writing reference books, take a class, go to a conference, and otherwise do professional development while you wait for the results of your submission round. This is also worthwhile to do during the odd limbo period before a book is released into the world.

AUTHOR PLATFORM CHECKLIST

Here's what else you can be doing while on submission or alongside your active writing.

01 Develop strong follow-up projects, whether part of a series or meant to stand alone. ☐

02 Pursue placing articles or short pieces in blogs, literary magazines, online journals, and/or trade magazines. This bolsters your professional experience, as expressed in your query bio. ☐

03 Develop a strong informational website.
Here's what to include:

☐ Static **homepage** with info about you

☐ **About** page with links to clips/published work

☐ **Projects** page with short summaries

☐ **Contact** page (with a form or email link)

☐ **Blog** (optional, and only if you can be consistent)

04 Nurture your social media footprint, or at least create some profiles for your brand on X/Twitter, Instagram, TikTok, etc. ☐

05 Take classes and attend conferences or writing events, if available to you. ☐

06 READ! READ! READ! ☐

---

07 Practice pitching your work at events or online so that you're always putting yourself out there. Virtual conferences make this easier, in terms of both time and budget. ☐

---

08 Patronize local literary events. Get a feel for your immediate writing community. ☐

---

09 Participate in message boards and forums. Contribute to threads and build up a following in online writing groups. Consider my interactive online learning program and community, **Writing Craft Workshop**! ☐

KEEP GOING!

The publishing marketplace, literary agent responses, and sales numbers are largely out of your control. Your own commitment to your work, learning your craft, and pushing the boundaries of your creativity, however, are always within reach.

You don't always have to either be writing or going on submission, either. Especially if you just queried, it can be compassionate to take a breather and plan your next steps. Sometimes it helps to remember why you love writing, and stop chasing the outcome of a published book. ("Progress, not product.") There is no right way to approach these topics.

Focus on your self and your creative intention as you forge your way forward as a writer, no matter what happens in the slush pile.

CONCLUSION

Writing a book allows you to leave your mark on the world. The things you have to say while expressing yourself creatively are some of the most essential and important ideas you might ever share.

Writing is an opportunity and a responsibility, and your readership deserves nothing but the best. The great part is, as a creative writer, you get to go on one heck of a quest yourself, in order to take your reader on a journey of their own.

You are a work in progress, as is your, well, work in progress! The market is constantly shifting. As it does, you can be honing yourself, your author identity, your brand, your message, and your writing skill.

As you craft your pitch, you will hone your premise, which will focus your pitch. Writing is a lifelong endeavor, so commit to the journey and get out there!

Kole

MARY KOLE

RESOURCES

In addition to the submission resources on pages 122 and 123, here are some useful articles for you. These mostly come from my writing and publishing blog, Kidlit, but are evergreen and don't only apply to children's books. These articles appear in no particular order.

"Types of Rejection Letters and Query Rejection"
- https://kidlit.com/types-of-rejection/

"How to Write a Novel Synopsis"
- https://kidlit.com/write-novel-synopsis/

"How to Write a Query Letter"
- https://kidlit.com/how-to-write-a-query-letter

"Query Letter Plot Pitch: Premise vs. Plot"
- https://kidlit.com/plot-pitch/

"Concrete Writing: Using Specific Language"
- https://kidlit.com/concrete-writing/

"Comp Titles and Other Questions About Book Comps"
- https://kidlit.com/comp-titles-in-a-query-book-comps/

"How to Write a Picture Book Query"
- https://kidlit.com/picture-book-query/

"Your Query Letter Hook and Revealing the Ending"

- https://kidlit.com/query-letter-hook

"Comparative Titles in a Query"

- https://kidlit.com/comparative-titles/

"Finding Comp Titles"

- https://www.goodstorycompany.com/blog/finding-comp-titles/

"Writing a Proactive Protagonist"

- https://kidlit.com/writing-a-proactive-protagonist/

"Should I Copyright My Book Before Sending it To a Publisher?"

- https://kidlit.com/should-i-copyright-my-book-before-sending-it-to-a-publisher/

Submission Tracker Spreadsheet

- https://bit.ly/subspreadsheet
- This resource is a Google Sheet (a cloud-hosted spreadsheet)
- Go to "File" and then "Make a copy …" to repurpose it for yourself on your own Google Drive.

Writing Blueprints Submission Resource:

If a deep dive into the submission process sounds helpful, my self-paced course contains over ten hours of instruction. There will definitely be some information overlap between the class and this workbook, but you'll also get access to agent interviews, over thirty handouts, and a comprehensive step-by-step submission guide.

https://bit.ly/kolesub

OFFERINGS FOR WRITERS

Since 2009, I've been creating educational materials for writers and designing courses, books, and services on writing and publishing topics. I regularly teach free webinars about query letters, character, plot, and first pages. Some webinars offer the opportunity for live feedback, including your query.

Please check out a current list of my upcoming workshops here:

https://goodstorycompany.com/workshops

I'm also available to Zoom into your critique group or design a presentation or workshop for a writing retreat or conference.

WORK WITH ME

If you enjoyed this workbook, consider getting personalized one-on-one advice from me. My specialty is deep developmental editing on your entire manuscript, though I love working on query letters and submission materials as well. Alternatively, I am happy to step in as a ghostwriter or offer ghost revision for your project. We can also work together in a small group writing workshop intensive setting.

SERVICES

Developmental Editing Services:

https://marykole.com

Ghost Revision and Ghostwriting Services:

https://manuscriptstudio.com

Story Mastermind Small Group Writing Workshops:

https://storymastermind.com

GOOD STORY COMPANY

In 2019, I created Good Story Company as an umbrella brand so that my amazing team and I could collaborate in the service of writing and writers. GSC is where you'll find our most comprehensive library of resources and services.

Good Story Company:

https://goodstorycompany.com

Good Story Podcast:

https://goodstorypodcast.com

Good Story YouTube Channel:

https://youtube.com/goodstory

Writing Craft Workshop Membership:

https://www.goodstorycompany.com/membership/

Good Story Marketing:

https://goodstorycompany.com/marketing

BEFORE YOU GO...

If you enjoyed this workbook, there are **three small things** you can do which would make a big difference to me and Good Story Company. Thank you so much for your time, kind attention, and consideration!

Subscribe to Our Newsletter

Our respectful, short, and non-spammy newsletter features all of our latest and greatest resources, workshops, events, and critique opportunities. Go here to sign up:

https://bit.ly/hellogsc

Leave an Honest Review

Please also consider leaving a review for this title with your retailer of choice, as well as Goodreads. I love getting feedback of my own, and testimonials help greatly with our discoverability and marketing efforts, so that we can reach more writers.

Reach Out

Finally, I'd love to hear your experience and celebrate your accomplishments. If you run into some trouble in the writing and publishing worlds, don't be a stranger, either. Drop me a line:

mary@goodstorycompany.com

ALSO BY MARY KOLE

*Writing Irresistible Kidlit: The Ultimate Guide to Crafting Fiction
for Young Adult and Middle Grade Readers*

*Writing Irresistible Picture Books: Insider Insights Into Crafting
Compelling Modern Stories for Young Readers*

Writing Irresistible Picture Books Workbook

*Irresistible Query Letters: 40+ Real World Query Letters
with Literary Agent Feedback*

*How to Write a Book Now: Craft Concepts, Mindset Shifts, and Encouragement to
Inspire Your Creative Writing*

Writing Interiority: Crafting Irresistible Characters

Made in United States
Troutdale, OR
11/07/2024